Pandemic:
A Test of the News

Pandemic:
A Test of the News

Alan O'Connor

Winchester, UK
Washington, USA

JOHN HUNT PUBLISHING

First published by Zero Books, 2022
Zero Books is an imprint of John Hunt Publishing Ltd., No. 3 East St., Alresford,
Hampshire SO24 9EE, UK
office@jhpbooks.com
www.johnhuntpublishing.com
www.zero-books.net

For distributor details and how to order please visit the 'Ordering' section on our website.

Design: Stuart Davies

UK: Printed and bound by CPI Group (UK) Ltd, Croydon, CR0 4YY
Printed in North America by CPI GPS partners

We operate a distinctive and ethical publishing philosophy in
all areas of our business, from our global network of authors to
production and worldwide distribution.

Contents

Alan O'Connor is Professor of Media Studies at Trent University in Canada. He has written and edited three books about Raymond Williams and two books on community radio in Latin America. His most recent book describes punk-rock record labels in the 1990s as an example of what Pierre Bourdieu calls an artistic field.

Preface

This book was researched during the first wave of the pandemic, under lockdown in Toronto. It was written in the gaps between days of online teaching (I don't use Zoom for ethical reasons) in the second wave that Ontario experienced in early 2021. Now in a third wave, the radio has afternoon phone-in shows in which distressed listeners describe family members dead, ordinary life suspended, a confused roll-out of vaccines, and (for some people) unavoidable risk. The radio host is sympathetic but carefully keeps the talk to personal issues of survival.

A year into the pandemic, there is some radical questioning in the mainstream media. The *New York Times* has not forgotten about systemic inequality and the scandal of Amazon warehouse workers.[1] The *Globe and Mail* is investigating the lack of preparedness for a pandemic. The *Toronto Star* has investigative reporting on nursing homes. There is news of disaster in India. But this tends to get lost in newspapers that clearly want business as usual: sports, entertainment, fashion, weddings, real estate.[2]

Where I live, in Ontario, there is some realization that the government was all along acting on behalf of business interests and not 'the people'. Asked to divert vaccines to racialized neighbourhoods in Toronto that have stunning rates of positive tests, the premier said it would mean taking vaccines away from seniors. Asked to take meaningful steps in factories, Amazon warehouses and meat-packing plants, the premier announced new police powers to stop and question anyone on the street. (The police mostly declined.) It took local public health officers to shut down factories and warehouses that have more than five cases of Covid-19 over a 14-day period. Why was this not done a year ago?

Mainstream news media could pursue a line of radical

questioning. It is noticeable that doctors who are critical of the government are given more space to speak out. A small number of books and 'long reads' explore fundamental issues about what caused the pandemic, cutbacks to public health and delays in governments taking the outbreak seriously in January 2020. But the news media jumps from story to story: Zoom bombs and mobile-phone tracing apps are old news. The story today is where to get a vaccine, tips about personal survival and talk about when this is all over.

There are some critical voices. Will this develop into a radical questioning of the state? Gramsci describes this as a crisis of hegemony. This kind of political crisis is often precipitated by incompetent handling of a natural disaster (the 1972 earthquake in Nicaragua) or the loss of a war (the war between Bolivia and Paraguay in the 1930s). There are news reports that describe the state's incompetent response to the pandemic. The government responds with public relations and in Ontario resumes attacks on teachers' unions. It is not yet the moment to attack the nurses' associations, though no long-term pay increase is offered. The state has other powers. The police in Ontario were for several months given access to lists of people who tested positive for Covid-19. More recently Premier Ford wanted to give the police sweeping powers to stop people, force them to give their name, address and explain why they were not at home. These powers still exist for any organized protest on the streets. The premier likes to talk tough: 'I have never hesitated to act.' Gramsci insisted that a crisis in political hegemony could go either way, a progressive outcome and fundamental social change ought not be assumed. It all depends on preparation (Gramsci calls this a war of position) and there are some signs of this: a militant anti-racist movement, young people outspoken about climate change. Against this there is widespread apathy about digital surveillance, and many young people say they do not read newspapers.[3]

Introduction

The first phase of the Covid-19 pandemic lasted from mid-March to the end of May 2020.[4] This short book examines how mainstream news media responded to the emergency. The pandemic pushed the environmental crisis and forest fires off the front pages of our newspapers.[5] The viral pandemic dominated the news until the police killing of George Floyd on 25 May, and the Black Lives Matter protests in the days that followed. Several other studies also comment on the heightened news coverage of Covid-19 from March to May 2020.

This book is based on a close reading of news websites of the *Globe and Mail*, the *Toronto Star*, *The Guardian* (North American edition) and the *New York Times*. It also includes an analysis of CBC news videos from March to May 2020. The field of Canadian news is relatively autonomous, but in a world of online websites it also competes with international news organizations. People in Canada are generally interested in local news and the pandemic played out differently in Canada than in the United States. Nonetheless, Canadians also read newspapers such as the *New York Times* and magazines such as the *New Yorker*. Canadians with family abroad might look at the *Irish Times*, or even a local newspaper such as the *Pensacola News Journal*, for news affecting family members. This book also takes a look at online news sites such as VICE News and conservative sources such as Fox News.

The general finding is that mainstream news media, excluding Fox News, did a good job in informing citizens about the virus and measures to be taken to slow its spread (social distancing, hand-washing, wearing a mask). By other measures, news media were not as successful. There was little investigative reporting into the fundamental issues. In many countries, political leaders were permitted to frame the issues and were seldom challenged by journalists. The situation in the United States was somewhat different and is discussed in Chapter 2. To go beyond the headlines, a careful reader would need to turn to an in-depth article in the *New Yorker,* or to *The Guardian* (available online with no paywall), which published a diversity of Opinion pieces by experts, and good coverage of the crisis in the Global South. The *New York Times* expanded its sphere of legitimate news topics by covering issues of social class in the pandemic and generally questioning the line taken by the Trump Administration. The Pandemic was a difficult test for the media and there is no doubt that news organizations with deep resources performed better. New media such as VICE News has occasional scoops. The website has many reports on Covid-19, some of them quite good, but VICE lacks the resources to compete with organizations such as the *New York Times* and *The Guardian*.

Chapter 1

The Original Test of the News

In 1920 the American journalist Walter Lippmann published (with Charles Merz and Faye Lippmann) an examination of news reports in the *New York Times* about the 1917 Russian Revolution. The *New York Times* had by then established itself as the newspaper of record in the United States. But Lippmann and Merz concluded that from the point of view of professional journalism, the reporting on the Russian Revolution was nothing short of a disaster. On all essential questions it was misleading. The political elite that read the *Times* for information and perspective on what was happening in Russia was seriously misled.[6]

The issue was not simply one of facts. The problem is the frame in which the news is presented. Because the *New York Times* as an organization, founded on middle-class business and professional values, could not imagine that an anti-capitalist revolution might succeed. The narrative in the *Times* was that a madcap revolution was being attempted by extremists in Russia and this revolution had no chance of success. The problem was not that the *Times* got the facts wrong. The problem was not misinformation. Lippmann and Merz describe a media frame or narrative that simply could not imagine that a revolution might take place in Russia.

This kind of study of the news is continued by many books, perhaps most famously by Edward Herman and Noam Chomsky in *Manufacturing Consent* (originally published in 1988). They offer an institutional analysis of five factors which explain why the *New York Times* is propaganda for the ruling elite. Their institutional analysis describes:

1. ownership of news media, mostly by large for-profit corporations
2. the long-term effects of relying on advertising to fund newspapers
3. the ways in which government and corporate public relations shape the news
4. flak from conservative organizations aimed at reporters who question the status quo
5. radical reporters are accused of being communists and anti-American

In their case studies, they sometimes use a comparative method of paired examples. They find examples of similar behaviour such as human rights abuses by a nation state that is friendly to the USA and one that is deemed an enemy by the USA. They show that the friendly state's bad behaviour gets much less coverage, reports are held to a high standard of proof, and excuses are made. The enemy state is treated quite differently. Its misdeeds are repeatedly reported at length, any evidence is printable, and the state is roundly condemned.[7]

Media institutions and reporters work in what the French

Figure 1: The journalistic field

Elite media not supporting political elite opinion

Elite media supporting political elite opinion

Popular media not supporting political elite opinion

Popular media supporting political elite opinion

sociologist Pierre Bourdieu calls the field of journalism. There is a diversity of media outlets. Herman and Chomsky mainly focus on elite newspapers such as the *New York Times*. These news outlets are important but many people also read magazines (print or digital), a wide diversity of websites, and local newspapers. Bourdieu's approach to the journalistic field is useful as a way of arranging different media outlets and their contents. Radical activists might be sceptical about an elite magazine such as the *New Yorker*, but in the Covid-19 pandemic it published some excellent in-depth journalism.

This approach to media as a field does not contradict Herman and Chomsky's institutional theory because it turns out that most media are found on the right side of the diagram. Bourdieu worries that the journalistic field is overly dependent on the field of political power. He calls for more autonomy for journalists and news organizations. Nonetheless it is worth noting that magazines (and occasionally newspapers) with sizeable circulations do provide conditions of work for correspondents who challenge the political elite of the day.[8]

Many people get their news online. Yochai Benkler and his associates describe this using large data sets of news stories on social media. In *Network Propaganda* they show that in the United States there is a right-wing media ecosystem which is insulated from other parts of the media network. Extreme websites (which do not follow journalistic norms) are accredited and amplified by Fox News. This makes up about one-third of the media system in the USA. Left or liberal websites (Huffington Post) are linked to traditional news sources (*New York Times*) and are held accountable to traditional journalistic norms. They operate in a different way than the right-wing media ecosystem.

It is important to understand that this is not caused by technology. The problem is not that the internet has a polarizing effect. It is not caused by social media algorithms or so-called filter bubbles. It is a matter of interactions between institutions, media ecosystems and political culture. Benkler does not blame social media, technology or the internet for destabilizing American society. 'It is only when the underlying institutional and political-cultural fabric is frayed that technology can exacerbate existing problems' (Benkler, *Network Propaganda*, p. 23).

American media is polarized because American society is polarized. A minority of American people (perhaps 30 percent of the population) feel that they have been abandoned by society. They seek out conservative politicians to voice their concerns. This continues a historical trend. From 1949 to 2011 voting patterns in the House of Representatives polarized. Today there is little overlap in voting patterns between Republicans and Democrats. Benkler argues that polarization among the public in the United States has little to do with the agenda and competence of politicians. Voters are mostly poorly informed about political matters. Polarization among conservative voters is expressed in emotional responses to the civil rights and feminist movements. Conservative sectors look to the media, not so much for facts and information, but for identity confirmation. Outrageous opinion gets the most attention.

These conservative sentiments are amplified by deregulated television and radio. Older and conservative voters rely more on traditional media than websites or social media. Network Propaganda gives a history of media organizations in the United States that is quite similar to the institutional analysis of Herman and Chomsky. Deregulation of the media industry from the 1980s allows for the emergence of conservative talk radio (Rush Limbaugh) and Fox News, which are no longer required to be fair and balanced. An isolated and conservative segment of the media ecosystem now caters for about 30 percent of Americans. This segment of the media system consists of conservative talk radio, Fox News and conservative websites such as the Drudge Report (founded in 1995) and Breitbart (started in 2007). These media operate in isolation from the rest of the media field. Conservative voters in the United States express high levels of trust in these media outlets.[9]

Chapter 2

Misinformation and Social Media

Awareness of Covid-19 hit North America in March 2020. Many people anxiously turned to television for news and information. There were also rumours and denials on the internet. Researchers on public opinion and in health communication rapidly produced studies of social media as a spreader of misinformation. By comparison with media studies described in the previous chapter, these studies have a very narrow focus. Nonetheless it will be useful to look at this research before turning to broader issues of how the pandemic is framed by mainstream news organizations.

A study by the Pew Research Center found that Americans who rely on social media for their news are less informed about the virus and how to prevent its spread, and report more frequently being exposed to misinformation.[10] Social media is often associated with youth, innovation and emerging technologies, but studies show that people who get their news on social media are poorly informed, exposed to misinformation and conspiracy theories about Covid-19 (such as the virus was deliberately released by China, Covid-19 is caused by electronic emissions), and more likely to believe misinformation. Those who get news on social media are low in what the sociologist Pierre Bourdieu calls economic and cultural capital. They are young, have lower levels of education and lower income. The levels of knowledge of those who get news on social media is similar to those who rely on local television, and much lower than those who read newspapers or visit news websites, or watch television network news.

Several studies show that Americans who rely on Fox News are more likely to believe that Covid-19 does not need to be taken seriously and these Americans are more likely to engage in risky behaviour such as not wearing masks and engaging in unnecessary travel.[11] A study of Canadian news found that exposure to Twitter is associated with misperceptions (about Vitamin C, Covid-19 caused by the consumption of bats, that Covid is no worse than the flu) while the inverse is true for readers of news media.[12] Other studies provide evidence that people who are exposed to misinformation are less likely to follow public health measures to limit the spread of the disease. Those exposed to misinformation are more likely to engage in unnecessary travel and risky social interactions. They are less likely to observe measures such as social distancing and wearing a mask.

From a health communication point of view this is bad news. Health communication is focused on transmitting information from medical experts to the general public. This is sometimes called administrative research. Problems with this kind of research include:

1. A reliance on sample surveys rather than other research methods such as in-depth interviews or ethnography;
2. The unreflexive use of categories such as race/ethnicity, education and income and a lack of a theory of cultural capital (Bourdieu) which might explain the results better;
3. An accumulation of research results that suggest media effects but actually show correlations rather than effects: a study by Romer and Jamieson concludes by saying that they cannot make strong causal claims;
4. Lack of attention to a large body of research about participatory communication in development and health education rather than 'information' provided in a top-down manner by experts and mass media;[13]
5. Research that excludes critical thinking about government sources (one of Herman and Chomsky's

institutional filters) and seeks to defend 'the integrity of the US government' (Jamieson and Albarracin);

6. A lack of critical thinking about social media corporations taking down misleading posts and videos. About the same time Twitter, Facebook and YouTube were doing this for misinformation about Covid-19, Zoom was closing down discussions about Tiananmen Square (at the request of the Chinese government) and the Palestinian struggle (at the request of several Jewish groups);

7. Difficulties in accessing databases held by social media corporations are treated only as a problem for the research rather than a broader issue of surveillance capitalism and the privatization of data by for-profit corporations;

8. Lack of a political economy perspective on media ownership and deregulation of news organizations since the 1980s, which is usually taken as a given.

All of these studies assume that the social problem is 'misinformation' rather than government policies for paid sick leave, for-profit nursing homes, decreased inspections of nursing homes, decreased spending on public health, lack of preparation for a pandemic leading to unavailability of testing for the virus, insufficient resources for contact tracing, failure to close down factories, meat-packing plants and warehouses, failure to prioritize high-risk communities (low income, racialized), failure to release low-risk prison inmates (including those awaiting trial). Is the main problem in the Covid-19 pandemic actually misinformation?

The concern about the 'politicization' of Covid-19 perhaps needs some further thought. It seems to rest on a fairly naive notion of science as existing outside of any social or political context. The concern is understandable: findings upon which there is a high degree of scientific consensus are being dismissed for reasons that have little to do with science. Nonetheless it is important to note some significant debates and differences: medical opinion that wearing a mask in everyday life is useless became advice to wear a mask; findings that the virus is spread by droplets is contested by research that seems to show aerosol transmission. The point here is not to dismiss science but to recognize that science is an activity that takes place over time. Even more striking, as the pandemic went on, the range of doctors permitted to speak in the media expands from government expert advisers to doctors willing to criticize government policies (lack of sick pay) and to advocate for social justice rather than simply medical treatment. Perhaps there are legitimate political issues in public health. Many experts in public health would say they are unavoidable.

Yochai Benkler and his research team move beyond this narrow focus on misinformation.[14] Their lengthy report on polarization and the pandemic examines the media frames or narratives about Covid-19. The question here is not just whether the media get the basic facts correct. Instead they focus on the ways in which media ecosystems gather and filter the news, create an interpretative lens and sustain a narrative about Covid-19. Their study examines narratives about the pandemic, such as putting the blame on China for originating the virus.

Following the method used in Benkler and others, *Network Propaganda*, they examine news items in proportion to media hyperlinks such as Facebook posts or tweets linking to the news item.[15] For example, an article by Laurie Garrett in *Foreign Policy* that was sharply critical of the Trump administration's partial dismantling of America's pandemic preparedness was widely shared on social media in February 2020.[16] The research describes how the American public is polarized about the pandemic and how this plays out in the 2020 electoral campaign. Conservative media, with Fox News functioning as a central node, selectively engages with mainstream media to defend Trump and play down the seriousness of the medical crisis. By May 2020 conservative media in the USA tacitly admit to the severity of the crisis but respond by changing the media topic to attacks on Barack Obama and Joe Biden.[17]

Problems with this research include:

1. The frame of the research is US electoral politics and especially the 2020 presidential election. By comparison, the *New Left Review* special issue (March/April 2020) on the pandemic includes perspectives from China, India, Indonesia, Brazil, Iran and Japan.

2. The emphasis on the US election diverts attention from topics such as media coverage of Covid-19 outbreaks in retirement homes, Amazon warehouses and meat-packing plants, the relation between social class and Covid-19, and the environmental aspects of transmission of the virus from animals to human beings.

3. It is surprising to see the *New York Times*, the *Washington Post*, CNN, NBC News and ABC News described as 'left-leaning media outlets' (Faris, p. 19) when there is a large body of leftist media research that is highly critical of these media. The researchers seem to consider genuinely leftist sources (*Jacobin*, *Tribune*, *New Left Review*) as beyond the sphere of legitimate controversy. Benkler elsewhere describes his research on the media ecosystem as primarily addressed to working journalists (and journalism students) who should at least be made aware of the full range of news sources, websites and leftist magazines.

Benkler and his team provide a sophisticated treatment of the US media ecosystem, its internal patterns of linking stories, and the role of Facebook and Twitter in disseminating news stories.

Apart from reports about numbers, such as maps of rates of Covid-19 infection in the United States, what circulates most on social media are strongly partisan items. This confirms Benkler's findings in *Network Propaganda* about a partisan division in the US media ecosystem between mainstream news and conservative news frameworks.

Research by Benkler and others suggests that the problem is not social media as a source of misinformation and outrageous opinions.[18] There is increasing evidence that this online material originates with dedicated organizations and social media accounts such as Breitbart, Infowars and Fox News. We know that a majority of people reject this material. Misinformation is tweeted, but it tends not to be retweeted. Rebuttals of misleading or outrageous material, including humorous responses, often have the effect of spreading the memes online. The suggestion that it be reported to Twitter, Facebook and YouTube as inappropriate material is useful. But it does not deal with the general problem of giving these corporations unilateral power to close down accounts. What other accounts will be closed down? Anarchists, climate activists advocating direct action, anti-capitalist organizations, union organizers at Amazon warehouses? The more general problem is that we have allowed a part of the public sphere to be privatized and controlled by corporations such as Facebook, Twitter and Google.

Chapter 3

Television Tells the Story

We have seen that from a health communication perspective the main emphasis is on misinformation. A broader media studies perspective will recognize that television news is more than information. Television news tells a story, or perhaps multiple stories, about Covid-19. It is not just information. It is a narrative about what is happening, the major actors, the dangers foreseen and the measures taken. Television also will tell the stories of ordinary people who are affected by the pandemic. A television producer might ask: what is the story here? By that they mean, why is this story important? What larger issue or problem does it illustrate? Is this story about communities at risk that are being ignored? Is this story about people taking action to help in practical ways?

The CBC is Canada's public broadcaster. Originally a network of radio stations, then also a chain of television stations, the CBC today integrates broadcasting with its website. The CBC provides extensive coverage of the Covid-19 crisis, pushing out over a hundred reports each day. On the CBC national radio programme about politics, *The House*, federal Minister of Health Patty Hajdu is asked about preparations for the Covid-19 outbreak. She admits that there were cutbacks to public health. Also that a Canadian liaison position in China, whose job was to monitor health issues, was allowed to remain unfilled. But the main frame of the interview is not systemic issues of public health but whether the Canadian government moved quickly enough in responding to the pandemic.[19]

Mike Crawley, CBC provincial affairs reporter, asks at a press conference held by Premier Doug Ford about the elimination of systemic inspections of nursing homes and their replacement by complaint-driven inspections. In 2019 systematic inspections were done for only 9 out of 620 nursing homes. Ford passes the question to his Minister of Long-Term Care, who replies that the change was made because it is a better use of resources. Although this is a crucial issue in covering the crisis in long-term care, the story is not given prominence by the news media, which at this time generally described Premier Ford as doing a good job handling the crisis.[20]

In each case we see a reporter attempting to launch a story. But it mostly doesn't go anywhere. Mike Crawley tries to launch a story about government cutbacks to inspections of nursing homes. This might lead to critical questions about preparedness for a viral pandemic in nursing homes, or even for a serious outbreak of flu in another year. But the story dies. This is in part because of the difficulty of explaining to listeners the difference between the two types of inspections and why this matters. But the real problem has to do with political power. At this point in the pandemic, Premier Ford is riding a wave of popular support. (President Trump also enjoyed high approval rates for his handling of the pandemic in March 2020.) People who previously criticized Ford's cuts to education and public services now thought he was doing a good job. Mike Crawley's story doesn't go anywhere because it doesn't fit this overall narrative. Ford is doing a good job.

What other stories did the CBC tell? What narratives did resonate with broadcast audiences? Let's look at the most popular CBC news items about Covid-19 for the period from March to May 2020.[21]

At the start of the crisis in March, CBC television news provides 3-minute updates (sometimes longer 12-minute reports) which focus on the number of new cases, include footage from Premier Ford's press conferences announcing new initiatives taken by the government (there is no critical questioning of the premier) and other spots news such as temporary problems with Telehealth Ontario. There is a segment from the press conference of a public officer of health and camera footage of empty streets in downtown Toronto. There is then a segment from the prime minister's daily press conference, announcing financial aid (there is some questioning of the prime minister) and a brief statement that the Canadian-US border remains closed to non-essential traffic.

The City of Toronto Public Health Officer at a press conference recommends that bars and restaurants close down and move to take-out only. Nightclubs, bars and cinemas should close. There are statistics on the number of new cases and evidence of community spread of the virus. There is footage from the premier's press conference announcing new legislation. The premier arrives on a stage with four officials and stands in front of a display of Ontario flags. He urges people that there is no need for panic-buying in the supermarkets. At the prime minister's press conference there is an announcement that the border will be closed to non-essential travellers. Canadian travellers should come home immediately.

There is an emphasis on case numbers (Mike Davis in his review of media coverage speaks of a chaos of numbers), deaths in long-term residences (with a visual of a hand-made sign thanking the staff), statements from health officials at press conferences announcing steps to be taken: everyone is urged to do their part. Non-essential businesses will close. There is an interview in the street with a tattoo-shop owner. Construction sites will remain open (there is no comment on this). A medical expert is interviewed who says that the list of businesses permitted to remain open is probably too long and should be adjusted over time. There is camera footage from inside a supermarket and a report about grocery store workers on the front line in this crisis (at this time only some stores provide masks and plexiglass barriers). The union representing grocery store workers has called for more protection for the workers.

The union president is interviewed from his home. There is mention of the SARS epidemic in Toronto which did not require these kinds of measures. There is footage from inside a homeless shelter of bunk beds crowded together and a press conference by a City of Toronto official about a second case of Covid-19 in a shelter. The Ontario government will provide a financial update tomorrow (rather than a full-scale Budget) and it is expected to address economic aspects of the pandemic. There is a clip from the premier's press conference announcing reduced electricity rates for the next 45 days. The weather announcer urges viewers to enjoy the sunny weather in a responsible way.

By April 2020, the general parameters of the story are better understood. Canada's Chief Public Health Officer in a press conference describes some technical details about tests for the virus (each test performs somewhat differently) and problems of false positives and negatives. It is therefore premature to think about immunity passports. The CBC website directs us to the latest updates on the pandemic.

At his daily press conference, standing outside his official home, the prime minister responds to a journalist's question about export restrictions imposed by President Trump. The prime minister says that 3M understands how important it is to continue exporting N95 masks to countries like Canada. For several days, the Canadian government has been making the point to various levels of the American Administration that trade goes both ways across the border. In a follow-up question (each journalist is allowed one) she asks about the available supply of these masks in Canada. The prime minister is confident about the supply. A number of Canadian companies have stepped up and a supply is being arranged internationally. We will make sure that no part of Canada faces a shortage of medical supplies in this pandemic.

In late April, Nunavut sees its first confirmed case. The parliamentary budget officer predicts a $250B deficit. The CBC has dramatic footage of a flood in Fort McMurray. A woman describes how her house is flooded and she has no insurance because it is located on a flood plain. Some social distancing rules had to be relaxed in the response to the flood. A hotel that was closed down is now housing refugees. A girl is interviewed who says she has her books and computer for online classes (she is doing well in them). There is footage from a press conference by the Premier of Alberta who says he is encouraged to see that volumes of water are starting to go down. The reporter concludes that the people of Fort McMurray will face this together.

By early May infections are starting to decline in Ontario; but there is an outbreak of Covid-19 at a Quebec meat-processing facility. The CBC has a report about Mother's Day. A woman visits her mother's grave with just her granddaughter. She was a great lady. However, other graveyards are closed. There are images of young people running outside and on bicycles. At a press conference, British Columbia's provincial health officer advises physical distancing and exercise outside. She urges people to honour older people by keeping them safe. There are family photos of an elderly woman, and her family speak into the camera, wishing her a happy day. The studio announcer reads a displayed tweet saying that today my mom is helping people at Roland McDonald House.

In late May there is a report about large crowds that gathered in Trinity Bellwoods Park on Saturday. Mobile-phone videos show groups of young people sitting on the lawn. A studio reporter says that Toronto residents are outraged to see these images from the park yesterday. Some of the groups are larger than five people, the maximum allowed. Bye-law officers did not take any action because there were only six officers on duty. Ontario is seeing an uptick in Covid-19 cases and this is concerning to doctors and public health officers. A doctor is interviewed from his office. He asks if these are family members in the park and points out that Covid-19 is now a community-spread thing. The current uptick is due to Mother's Day gatherings and there is concern about what we will see in 2 weeks. The studio announcer points out that this is taking place just as the economy is starting to open up. A doctor is interviewed, who speaks emotionally about how he is not celebrating Eid (he explains that for him it is similar to Christmas), but he is working today in the hospital and dismayed to see these large gatherings of people.

A report on CBC, The National in May describes the effects of the pandemic on low-income Canadians. There is an interview with a family in Winnipeg. The children play ball in the street. A woman says that we are struggling, being cramped in a small house. We are not allowed to go to any of the playgrounds. Video footage of swings blowing slightly in the wind. The fine for using the playground is almost $500 and that's half a month's grocery money. For those of us living pay-cheque to pay-cheque, we're struggling. School at home is also a struggle. The family has only one computer and has to print out worksheets for the children. The woman says she can't order take-out food or watch Netflix. She is struggling to make ends meet.

Figure 2: CBC News reminds viewers about the rules

CBC News · Posted: May 24, 2020 7:02 AM ET | Last Updated: May 25, 2020

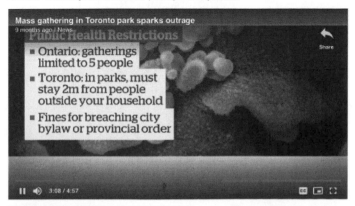

Thousands gathered in Trinity Bellwoods Park on Saturday, sparking a wave of anger online. City officials say the gathering is unacceptable. 4:57

By mid-May 2020 Canadian provinces were starting to reopen their economies. There was some debate about this. An edition of *Power & Politics* in mid-May includes interviews with two doctors who stress the need for more widespread testing for the virus and more consistency in policies between the provinces. The relative of a patient in an Ontario long-term care home says that more staff are needed. When they call on the kitchen staff to do the work of a personal support worker, that is an indication that more staff are needed. The CBC website provides updates, statistics, maps and graphs of case numbers, and sometimes videos of provincial press conferences. In late May, *The National* shows garden centres and sporting goods shops reopening but public health officials are worried about a second wave. Case numbers in Ontario and Quebec are still quite high.

The CBC does a good job of informing viewers about the basic facts. There is an emphasis on statistics. Covid-19 is caused by a virus and needs to be taken seriously.[22] To reduce its spread the public is asked to social distance and limit social gatherings to immediate households. The CBC uses footage from official press conferences but there is no critical questioning of political leaders. The impression is that they are doing a good job of handling the crisis. We are shown the impact of the pandemic on the lives on doctors and ordinary people. But in the sample we have reviewed there is no investigative reporting that challenges the public-relations frame established by political leaders in Canada.[23]

Chapter 4

Behind the Headlines

Studies of news media and previous pandemics emphasize that the issue is not simply whether newspapers get the basic facts correct. The issue is the media frame or narrative.[24] For example, a study of the 2009 influenza H1N1 pandemic finds that the media frame starts by raising the alarm, then offers a mix of fearful and reassuring stories (we have to fight this enemy), and finally a frame about containment.[25]

Another study of news frames of the H1N1 flu pandemic shows how journalists turn official press releases into news stories.[26] The research looks at the *Straits Times*, the newspaper of record in Singapore, a more authoritarian capitalist system than the United States. Although journalists are heavily dependent on official press releases for information, they also select from press releases and provide interpretative frames for the pandemic. Many press releases are quite routine and do not result in a printed news story. The main categories of stories deal with basic information (such as the number of cases) and preventive information (hand-washing, taking temperature). However, at least half of the stories go beyond these basic issues and seek to show the relationships between the medical emergency and societal and structural factors. Once journalists believe that readers have a grasp of the basic issues, they seek to write stories that place the emergency in a broader context. The education and backgrounds of reporters play a role in how they frame these stories. Will the story be about the impact of the pandemic on tourism, or will it place the pandemic in a broader context of irresponsible industrial capitalism and make a link to the climate warming crisis? Singapore is an authoritarian capitalist society. A reporter might write a story about social and political aspects of the H1N1 pandemic but will not question the overall system of capitalist development.

We can see a similar emphasis in how the Covid-19 pandemic is reported. A content analysis of coverage in the *Wall Street Journal*, the *New York Times* and *USA Today* from January to March 2020 found that the most frequent topics were the financial impact of Covid-19 (11.6 per cent), stories of affected individuals (7.0 per cent), deaths and death rates (6.8 per cent), precaution recommendations for the public (6.2 per cent) and quarantine (5.9 per cent). The emphasis on the economy and the financial impact of Covid-19 in the *Wall Street Journal* is not surprising. In more than 5000 articles from three newspapers in the early period of the pandemic, only a tiny fraction of articles are about social inequities (a total of 21 news stories).[27]

Examples of media frames

The first frame, or narrative, is a simple denial that Covid-19 exists. This is increasingly difficult to sustain but can be found online and in publications that claim that Covid-19 is a fabrication of 'liberal media.' In other words, Covid-19 is fake news. In the United States this is sometimes accompanied by an argument that Covid-19 is a myth invented to disrupt Donald Trump's campaign for re-election in 2020.[28]

The second frame, quite widespread in March 2020, is that the disease is trivial and does not need to be taken seriously. Prayer, piety or American masculinity are enough to end the disease. Donald Trump says that he had Covid and it is not so bad. Another version of this is various 'cures', which range from the anti-malaria drug hydroxychloroquine, touted by Trump as a possible 'game changer', to vitamins, and folk medicines which

---

boost the immune system.

A third frame diverts attention by blaming the outbreak on China (Trump wanted to call it the China Virus), making outrageous demands that China pay reparations for damaging the US economy, and in some cases claiming that the virus was released, deliberately or accidentally, by a research lab in China. This last version can be found in mainstream news and conservative writers such as James Rickards.[29]

The fourth frame, very widely found in mainstream news media, considers the disease to be caused by a foreign agent that appears out of nowhere. It is an unknown and unpredictable bug. This is usually accompanied by uncritically repeating politicians' statements that this is completely unprecedented, that nobody could have seen this coming. This frame diverts attention from previous outbreaks (SARS, H5N1), expert warnings about a future pandemic, government reports about the need to prepare for a future pandemic, and the lack of preparations in 2019-2020 as Covid-19 emerged.[30]

The fifth frame, known as One Health, shifts the emphasis from a virus to the ecological conditions that make it possible for viruses to jump from animal or bird reservoirs to humans. In many versions there is an intermediary animal (perhaps a small carnivore). This frame stresses the co-existence of humans and animals in a changing environment. This may involve the loss of forest habitat which brings together animals that previously did not interact. This frame mostly appears as a 'long read' in publications such as the *New Yorker* or *The Guardian*.[31]

The sixth frame stresses the historical role of globalized capitalism in shaping One Health. In this frame, it is the pressure from capitalism that places such stress on the complex relations between human / animal / environment that it makes global catastrophe almost certain. This frame is found only in small-circulation radical publications, or academic journals. Mainstream news never accepts this frame. The mainstream media repeats statements by politicians about the need to maintain 'the supply chain' at all costs, when in a longer timeframe this chain (other concepts are used) is actually responsible for the pandemic. This perspective is found in books such as Alex Blanchette's study of the pork industry and in the work of Robert G. Wallace. For mainstream news media it is literally unthinkable, just as the Russian Revolution was unthinkable for the *New York Times*, a hundred years ago.[32]

A year later the media frame has changed. It is now quite usual to find the pandemic discussed in terms of social inequality. There is clear understanding that the effects of the pandemic are unequally distributed. Disadvantaged communities have been most affected. Low-income workers in warehouses, transport and retail cannot work from home. Personal support workers are especially vulnerable, poorly paid and often from racialized backgrounds. The roll-out of vaccines privileged middle-class people who have the time and internet skills to obtain a booking, and time off work to drive to a vaccines centre. Issues of global inequality are not just a matter of social justice: the explosion of the pandemic in India and Brazil threatens the recovery of every society.

This book is based on careful reading of items related to Covid-19 on media websites, with an emphasis on the period from 15 March to 31 May 2020. This comparative approach also provides criteria for evaluating articles and reports. One of the best overviews of the crisis is an article in the *New Yorker* in May. This profile of Ali Khan at the Center for Disease Control describes how zoonotic viruses jump from animals (where they normally do no harm) to humans and how important it is to monitor viruses that appear likely to make the jump. SARS in 2002-03 is a key example and in many ways was a prior warning of the Covid-19 outbreak. SARS was highly infectious and a wake-up call about the necessity of early warning systems for any future outbreak of a similar virus.[33] Another article in the *New York Times Magazine* in April focused on the lack of interest by major drug companies in vaccine research and government cutbacks on research spending.[34] These and other articles provide a measure by which we may judge the media. Excellent reporting is often not the most widely circulated on social media, which pushes controversial and emotional items rather than long reads that carefully explain fundamental issues.

From 15 March to 31 May 2020, each of these news sites was read on a daily basis: the *Toronto Star*, *Globe and Mail*, *New York Times* and *The Guardian*. In order to situate these media in the larger field the following traditional news sites were also monitored: the *Irish Times*, as an example of a newspaper in a small country, and the *Pensacola News Journal*, as an example of a local paper in the United States. VICE News was regularly consulted as an example of new media. This was supplemented by a review of two magazines: the *New York Review of Books* and the *New Yorker*. Finally, as an example of conservative news sites, Fox News and Breitbart were monitored.[35]

Much of the coverage in the mainstream media is straightforward 'spot' news and this is probably what most people read on social media: live updates. This is a useful service about developments, statistics about cases, reports about hospitals, testing and tracing. Other items are 'news you can use' or lifestyle items about coping with lockdowns, dealing with children at home, cooking tips and advice for avoiding the virus.

What about in-depth reporting? The long reads that provide background and analysis, and also opinion pieces by experts and well-known writers. Studies of media have called for more of this kind of extended coverage, which is more expensive and time-consuming to produce than news updates and lifestyle tips. The standard here is news media as a public service, informing but also challenging and educating readers about multiple aspects of the coronavirus pandemic. This should include international coverage, especially of the global South, which tends to be marginalized in mainstream news media. This coverage is expensive to produce and it is often said that readers are not much interested in it.

The chaos of numbers

Following journalistic conventions of factual and objective reporting, all news media give daily counts of the number of Covid infections and deaths from the disease. These raw statistics give some information but are of limited value. Mike Davis speaks about a 'chaos of numbers'.[36] It is now known that many people who get infected are never tested or diagnosed. And the statistics of deaths exclude those who die as collateral effects of the Pandemic, such as increased deaths from cancer and drug overdoses. Statisticians are, of course, aware of these effects. Comparative statistics are more significant: Ontario, with its testing and medical system, has perhaps 800 new daily Covid-19 cases in Spring 2020 and with more or less the same system in place, over 3000 daily cases in January 2021. Statisticians would also use an array of measures, such as the rate of positive tests (there is a significant difference between having 1-percent positive tests and 12-percent positive tests). Maps showing the difference in rates between working-class and middle-class areas of the city display more meaningful information. Newspapers did provide such maps but the emphasis was always on the raw statistics which have limited value.

Controversy over contact-tracing apps

The issue of contact tracing for people carrying the virus received considerable attention but the main story was the value of smartphone apps for this purpose. To some extent this distracted attention from cutbacks to public health budgets that left these organizations without the capacity to rapidly upscale contact tracing by telephone. This follows journalistic conventions of framing an issue in terms of a simple and dramatic conflict: between supporters of these apps and privacy advocates who argue that the mobile-phone apps violate basic human rights to privacy. The details of how these apps actually work (some measure the strength of Bluetooth signals that were never intended to be used in this way) and the privacy measures enacted in some jurisdictions are more difficult to explain. Simplified and emotional arguments dominate on social media: for or against.[37]

The more significant issue is that this debate reduces what Pierre Bourdieu calls the social *habitus* to 'contacts'. This kind of thinking is prevalent in the world of computer programming: people and social life reduced to networks of contacts. (It perhaps describes something of the world of these computer professionals, multiple brief contacts at work, visits to hip coffee shops and casual urban encounters. In the general population, 50 percent of older Canadians do not even have a smartphone.) It is much more difficult for a journalist to understand and describe the *habitus* in which people actually live: their homes and families, neighbourhoods, daily routines of travel, their work in shops and factories. These are not 'contacts' but patterns of the social, which actually constitutes the determinants of health. The manufactured issue of contact-tracing apps has the effect of distracting attention from the social determinants of health, which get much less space in the news at this time.[38]

Zoom bombs

Zoom is widely used as an emergency video-meeting app in the early days of the pandemic in March 2020. Security problems with the app were widely reported. The design of Zoom permitted unauthorized users to disrupt meetings, sometimes with racist and abusive language. Reporting on this follows the pattern of mainstream news in exposing failures within the system. These might include politicians who are corrupt, or accept bribes. Or corporations and individuals who break existing laws and regulations; for example, a factory that releases contaminated waste into a river. In a similar way, Zoom was widely criticized in news media for marketing an app that had security problems. The company announced that it was concentrating all efforts on fixing these problems. The story ran its course and mainstream media moved on to other issues.[39]

A careful reader might notice that the problems are more fundamental. Security and privacy vulnerabilities with Zoom were known in 2018-19, but the company was slow to fix the problems. Most of its development budget went into making the app easy to use.[40] Interviews with Eric Yuan, Zoom's CEO, show his lack of engagement with security issues. His main emphasis is on ease of use of the service.[41] The problem is not just Zoom bombs. Zoom users who subscribed to a marketing service called LinkedIn Navigator could see LinkedIn profiles for people in Zoom calls. Privacy activists also discovered that Zoom was sharing user data with Facebook, even if users did not have a Facebook account. Zoom ended this practice in late March 2020 when it was threatened with a lawsuit.

Zoom software is developed in part in China (to save money) and in the early days of the pandemic, encryption keys for some users in North America were generated on servers located in China, making these accounts vulnerable to Chinese state surveillance. Zoom continues to use low-level encryption.[42]

Zoom was banned by many school boards, raising awareness of internet security (a teaching moment for students) because preventing Zoom bombs required IT expertise not available to most high-school teachers. In April 2020, governments around the world banned the use of Zoom for classified or confidential communication. Experts at the Citizen Lab, a research organization based in Toronto, repeat this warning. These cautions and warnings did little to halt the widespread use of Zoom during pandemic lockdowns when much work and social engagement went online. Zoom use increased dramatically. As the pandemic dragged on, Zoom stocks increased 400 per cent in value. Executives of the company sell company stock, increasing their personal wealth.[43] It is not illegal to profit from the pandemic, but this is a reminder that Zoom is not public space. It is owned and controlled by a for-profit corporation.

In June 2020, Zoom admitted to cutting off the accounts of political activists at the request of the Chinese government. Activists in North America and Hong Kong wanted to have a session about the 1989 Tiananmen Square protests. After some media coverage of this, Zoom apologized.[44] However, in November 2020 the corporation repeated the behaviour. It shut down a public university seminar with the Palestinian activist Leila Khaled, apparently at the request of several Jewish organizations. Zoom then cancelled online events organized at other universities that criticized how Zoom behaved. A spokesperson for Zoom said that the company reserves the right to bar anyone from using its services, for any reason.[45]

The issue here, as elsewhere in this book, is the frame in which the story is reported. Is the story about a corporation that marketed a faulty product, but then fixed the problems?

Or is this a larger issue of take-over of the public sphere by corporations such as Facebook, Twitter, Google and possibly Zoom? These corporations reserve the right to control expression on their platforms according to their terms of service. This is part of a larger problem of surveillance capitalism in which human activity and creativity is appropriated as data, owned and controlled by internet corporations.[46]

School at home

In March 2020 many countries imposed lockdowns. When much of life suddenly went online the inequalities in internet access became visible. But researchers have written about the digital divide for many years.[47] Figures for 'How Many Online' measure the population that has used the internet for 30 minutes in the past 30 days. The absurdity of this measure shows that the digital divide is a complex issue and involves issues of equipment (one laptop for three children taking online school lessons), speed and cost of internet access, skill in using the keyboard, skill in online search (advanced search options), and the education to evaluate and make effective use of information online. The digital divide was largely seen as an individual problem. One public figure in the United States said that there was also an expensive car divide: he wished he had one. Rather than being regarded as an issue of access to the public sphere, for political information and online job applications, it was regarded as a matter of individual consumer choices. With schools and colleges teaching online in the pandemic it now seems a matter of public policy.

Our sample of mainstream news includes 14 items from March to April 2020 about school at home. In mid-March 2020 schools closed as part of the general lockdown and learning went online. The families of journalists were affected along with everyone else and it is not surprising that experiences of online school are covered in mainstream news media. Students were asking questions about prom and graduation. From the start there were reports of social class differences: some students came to digital class meetings on time, others did not respond to texts, emails and social media blasts, and did not attend video meetings.[48] Some parents are able to help children with online learning, others lack language skills, education or time to help. There are problems of internet access in poorer neighbourhoods. There was some agreement that digital technology is no substitute for classrooms. In Italy it became apparent that dumping large amounts of homework on school children does not amount to an education.[49] By the end of April, the *Globe and Mail* was reporting that some parents were simply giving up on distance learning.[50] In May, Emma Beddington in *The Guardian* wrote about the mixed experiences of her children, including problems with the internet.[51] Cecilia Kang in the *New York Times* wrote about Americans without internet access, quoting the Pew Research Centre that one in four Americans have no high speed access at home, either because it is too expensive or because they live in a rural area. Teachers and students drove to parking lots where there is a Wi-Fi spot. As the weeks dragged on, there were reports of parents who began to lower expectations and reports often described differences between affluent and disadvantaged families.[52]

Disaster at long-term residences

Academic researchers have warned about conditions in nursing homes for years. A research group in Canada has documented employment conditions, physical buildings, the experiences of elderly people and public images of ageing. This research had little effect on public policies and the for-profit sector of long-term residences.[53]

Conditions in long-term care residences were also extensively covered in mainstream news in Spring 2020. In our sample there were more than 70 items. The news frequently reported a shortage of staff and lack of protective equipment. Many reports said that staff shortages and other problems had existed for years. In the United States the homes were frequently owned by for-profit corporations and got most of their income from Medicare and Medicaid. Some had been fined for providing substandard care in the past. The headlines were dramatic: 70 Died at a Nursing Home as Body Bags Piled Up (*New York Times*, 20 April 2020). Some of the reports describe personal experiences of residents and staff (usually speaking anonymously for fear of losing their jobs) but others are in-depth investigations done by teams of reporters.[54]

As previously discussed, the CBC reported that the Ontario government cut back on comprehensive annual inspections of long-term residences that included evaluation of preparations for a flu outbreak. Instead, the Ontario government substituted complaint-driven inspections which often deal with issues such as food and quality of care for individual patients. In Canada, long-term care homes were connected to 80 per cent of deaths from Covid-19. A CBC investigation found that the risk of dying from Covid-19 is significantly higher for residents of for-profit nursing homes. The *Toronto Star* also reported on this.[55]

Yet, the *Toronto Star* seemed hesitant to blame the Ontario government.[56] Even with a scathing report on conditions observed by the Canadian Armed Forces, which took over care in several nursing homes, the Ontario government was able to counter criticisms. (1) The difference between systemic and on-demand inspections of long-term residences has to be carefully explained by reporters. (2) The Ontario government announced a temporary pay increase for workers in long-term residences. (3) The government set up an independent commission to study long-terms residences, even though many studies already exist. (4) The Ontario government later promised 4 hours of daily care for each resident by 2024-25.

The *Toronto Star* regularly reports on deaths using vague language about 'staffing concerns' and challenges caused by the pandemic. An editorial in *The Guardian* uses more plain language: 'The government knew that elderly people were most vulnerable to Covid-19. But it failed to adequately shelter the social care sector.'[57] The Canadian news media gave little space to unions representing personal care workers and largely ignored half a dozen expert policy reports that were released in response to the crisis in nursing homes.[58]

Social determinants of health

A body of research in the field of public health predicted that a pandemic would affect marginalized populations and those living in poverty. In Canada, the work of Dennis Raphael over several decades has shown a relation between socio-economic status and health outcomes.[59] Children born in poverty weigh less at birth, and adults who live in poverty do worse for all major diseases, and they die earlier. Raphael provides maps of the city of Toronto showing the areas where visible minorities live. These are also the areas where rates of diabetes are highest. The maps are more or less the same for the areas of Toronto hit hardest by Covid-19 in 2020.[60]

In the initial period of the pandemic, news media was focused on the disaster in long-term care residences. But another story started to emerge. The pandemic was affecting some communities more than others. Rates of infection and death rates are higher in Afro-American neighbourhoods. Reports in the United States focused on disparities between Black communities and society in general. This was often framed by journalists as an issue of racialized inequality rather than social class, even when those interviewed described their situation in terms of work and social class: I have to work, I have to pay the rent, take public transit to work. The media in general was somewhat reluctant to adopt a frame about systemic inequality (including racialized inequality) and public health. It may be difficult to find, but is not completely absent from mainstream news.[61]

Dennis Raphael describes the reluctance of the media to adopt this perspective.[62] Members of the public generally believe that health outcomes are determined by genetics or lifestyle choices. They are surprised to discover that outcomes are actually determined by living conditions and social class. People think of tobacco use, exercise and diet but are surprised that systemic social factors actually determine health outcomes. Studies of media show that there are endless articles about healthy lifestyles but only a tiny number of articles about the social determinants of health. Reporters repeat the common sense about eating well and getting exercise but seem not to understand that health outcomes are not mainly a matter of individual choices. Newspapers have extensive food and lifestyle sections. Official reports on the social determinants of health are judged to be of little interest by media institutions. In the Covid-19 pandemic, this individualistic approach to thinking about health outcomes dominated in the early months. Very gradually, a more sociological approach to health outcomes began to appear in the news media.[63]

Critical reporting on Amazon

From April to June of 2020 there were over 40 news reports about Amazon in the *New York Times*, *Guardian*, *Globe and Mail* and *Toronto Star*. Many of these reports are critical accounts of conditions in Amazon warehouses, efforts of workers to organize and protest, and attempts by Amazon to smear workers and influence reporting about the company. One of the articles is a positive report about Amazon's sales and profits in the first quarter of 2020.

The BBC *Business Daily* on 16 April 2020 (carried by CBC Radio at 5am) was an in-depth report about Amazon. The company has been declared an essential service (and on its website says it is prioritizing essential goods), but warehouse workers report that apart from an increase in commodities such as cleaning supplies, it is pretty much business as usual (mention of a dog birthday cake). Apart from a few European countries, Amazon has no worker unions. There are reports of positive cases of Covid-19 in 50 warehouses. The pace of work to fulfil orders, pressure on workers and the imperative to meet orders as usual has not changed. Will Amazon provide sick leave? Extra cleaning of warehouses? Is Amazon disclosing cases of the virus? There is no independent monitor. Amazon is also a big tech company: it provides web services and entertainment streaming (including for video gamers). Jeff Bezos has announced he will donate $100 million to food banks. The BBC balanced claims by Dave Clark, Senior Vice President of Worldwide Operations at Amazon, on his blog that the protests are at a small number of sites and represent only a few hundred employees, with comments by Franklin Foer, author of *World Without Mind: The Existential Threat of Big Tech* (2017).[64]

The *New York Times* published about a dozen articles (for summaries see Appendix 3). The tone varies: a few are uncritical examples of access journalism which repeats corporate public relations, but most attempt to hold Amazon accountable. Some articles are quite critical of the way Amazon treats its employees and the corporation's secrecy about the number of Covid-19 cases at its warehouses. A few of these articles raise crucial issues about capitalism, the power of corporations such as Amazon and the unwillingness of the US government to defend workers' rights. On the whole, it seems quite unfair to call this propaganda for the ruling elite. It seems that in covering problems at Amazon in the early period of the pandemic, the 'sphere of legitimate controversy' expands and some writers at the *New York Times* are actually criticizing capitalism and the exploitation of workers. Nor did the *Times* abandon the story after the initial period of the pandemic. It regularly followed up the story from time to time, keeping it on the public agenda.[65]

Medical experts and social scientists warned about the possibility of a pandemic

Far from being unprecedented, the pandemic is similar to previous crises such as SARS in 2002-04, and the MERS outbreak from 2012. The virus that causes Covid-19 disease is named SARS-CoV-2 because it is related to (but also different from) the SARS virus. The HIV virus (symptoms of AIDS were first observed in 1981) is also a virus that jumped from an animal reservoir to infect human beings. Official reports on the SARS outbreak warned that a similar event was possible in the future. The SARS outbreak was contained mainly because patients were already seriously sick when they were contagious. The reports warned that a future virus could be much more difficult to manage.

Books were written. Mike Davis, *The Monster at Our Door: The Threat of Avian Flu* (2005), is by an urban theorist and historian. He offers a clear explanation of how viruses behave and the social and economic factors that make it possible for a virus to jump from an animal host (where it usually does no harm) to humans. Relentless economic development, the destruction of animal habitats, and poverty that causes people to look for new sources of protein are all factors. Industrially-farmed chicken replaces fish in the diet of the global poor. Environmental damage erodes natural barriers that contain viruses within an animal or bird reservoir. Davis warns that:

> The essence of the avian flu threat, as we shall see, is that a mutant influenza of nightmarish virulence — evolved and now entrenched in ecological niches recently created by global agro-capitalism — is searching for the new gene or two that will enable it to travel at pandemic velocity through a

densely urbanized and mostly poor humanity.

The twentieth century was no stranger to death by pandemics, and the poor and marginalized were most affected.[66] Governments could take precautions. But in the United States since the 1980s, conservative administrations have rebuffed calls by public health experts for action such as mass vaccine campaigns. Big pharmaceutical corporations were not very interested in the vaccine market prior to Covid-19. Most drug companies abandoned the field of vaccines. Social change such as crowding people into cities and the emergence of global supply chains created conditions for the rapid spread of a new virus. Neoliberal economic policies implemented just about everywhere since the 1980s call for reduced government spending on health. Public health budgets are especially vulnerable to cutbacks by conservative politicians elected to save taxpayers' money. The world was unprepared for the SARS outbreak in 2002. And the United States government was more concerned about terrorism and biological weapons than a possible viral pandemic.

Countries such as the United States, Canada and Great Britain had pandemic playbooks. Some had done field exercises to test preparedness for an infections disease outbreak.[67] Dr Theresa Tam became a familiar public health spokesperson in the Covid-19 emergency. She was also co-author of the *Canadian Pandemic Influenza Plan for the Health Sector*. An article in the *Globe and Mail* about this plan quoted federal health minister Patty Hajdu: 'Health systems were never designed for this kind of surge, I think federal governments for decades have been underfunding things like public health preparedness.'[68] In the United States there was the *National Strategy for Influenza Preparedness* (Homeland Security Council, 2005), followed by the *National Strategy for Pandemic Influenza Implementation Plan* (Homeland Security Council, 2006) and other reports including a recent *Pandemic Influenza Plan 2017 Update* (US Department of Health and Human Services, 2017). Political figures often refuse to answer questions about pandemic preparedness, or say this was something to be examined after the Covid-19 pandemic is over.

It is possible to read about all this in news media. It is more in investigative pieces in magazines such as the *New Yorker*, or long reads in the *New York Times* and *Guardian*. It is sometimes framed in terms of political responsibility. Leaders such as Donald Trump in the United States and Jair Bolsonaro in Brazil are roundly criticized in liberal media. Political leaders such as Justin Trudeau in Canada are criticized but in a more limited way, for failings in specific policies, or delays in purchasing vaccines. A conservative politician, Doug Ford in Ontario, gets some criticism but enjoys widespread approval (including in the news media) until the third wave in Spring 2021 exposes serious problems, mainly caused by policies that favoured corporations' desire for business as usual over issues of public health.

The New York Times expands its sphere of legitimate controversy

What conclusions can we come to from this survey? The first is somewhat surprising. At the *New York Times* there was an expansion of what Daniel Hallin, in his study of media coverage of the Vietnam War, calls 'the sphere of legitimate controversy'. It is quite astonishing, early in the crisis, to find the *New York Times* arguing for reform of the prison system in the United States. A healthy Afro-American man jailed for a non-violent drug offence was one of the first prison inmates to die from Covid-19. And to find quite extensive news coverage of working conditions at Amazon warehouses, including sympathetic reports about workers organizing. The *Times* published several in-depth investigations into nursing homes, reports that blame for-profit corporations and government agencies for the deaths. On 1 May, International Workers' Day, the *Times* published an Opinion piece by Chris Hughes making the case for a guaranteed basic income. The pandemic hit New York City hard and this resulted in an exodus of the wealthy and middle-class professionals from the city to summer homes and even to safer cities such as Boston. The *New York Times* published more than one exposé of this kind of class privilege. The most detailed report, by Kevin Quealy, drew on research based on mobile-phone data showing that the wealthiest New Yorkers quickly abandoned the city in mid-March 2020.[69]

Figure 3: Diagram from Dan Hallin (1989)

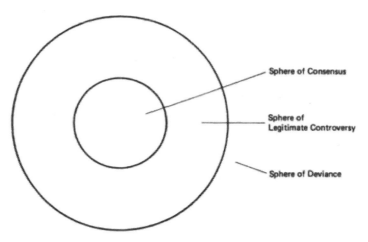

Figure 1 Spheres of consensus, controversy, and deviance.

There is a shelf of academic books criticizing the *New York Times*. Herman and Chomsky famously describe it as propaganda for the ruling elite. In the early 1900s the *Times* was unable to understand what was happening in the Russian Revolution. Why do we find these other periods in which the scope of the newspaper expands? Why in 2020? There are three answers. The first is that the *New York Times*, representing the opinion of the business and political elite in the USA, does not support Donald Trump, always regarded as an outsider by the elite. This gave the *Times* a critical perspective on President Trump's dismal performance on Covid-19. Second, the pandemic initially hit New York City hard. Reporters could see for themselves and experience in their own lives the effects of the Covid-19 pandemic. They wrote about what they saw. Third, a field theory of the media (Pierre Bourdieu) would explain the changes at the *New York Times* as a response to competition from the free online North American edition of *The Guardian*, a more liberal newspaper. There is some evidence for this. A series of articles in the *New York Times* under the rubric of 'The America We Need' attempts to imagine a better future after the pandemic. This series of articles seems to be modelled on a similar, but more robust, series of articles in *The Guardian*.

There are differences in the field of news media

The second conclusion from our survey of the news media in the initial months of the pandemic is that there are considerable differences between news organizations. The phrase 'mainstream news media' does not capture these significant differences. As previously argued, new media such as VICE News lack the deep resources of organizations such as the *New York Times* and *The Guardian*. The *Times* has approximately 1600 full-time journalists; VICE News has just 100 reporters.[70]

The most outstanding mainstream news organization in this period (continuing a pattern from before the crisis) is undoubtedly *The Guardian*. With offices in London, New York and elsewhere, and several different online editions, *The Guardian* has provided good reporting, thoughtful long reads and a wide range of Opinion pieces, often written by experts in different fields. *The Guardian* wrote about the crisis in developing countries and often tried to get at issues underlying the Covid-19 crisis such as inequality and the privatization of government services. *The Guardian* continued to publish articles on the environmental crisis, arguing that it is linked to the pandemic.[71]

Among magazines, the *New Left Review* published an insightful special issue on 'A Planetary Pandemic' and in the next issue, a key article by Robert Brenner, 'Escalating Plunder', about economic aspects of the pandemic in the United States.[72] The *New Yorker* published one of the best overviews about the virus, by David Quammen, and articles on the pandemic and social inequality.[73] The *New Yorker* website also published articles about Covid-19 in Afro-American communities and the effects of the Pandemic in India and other parts of the world.[74]

These publications should be situated in the left of the journalistic field. In the centre is mainstream news media including the *Toronto Star*, *Globe and Mail* (in Canada) and the *Irish Times*. There was much good reporting in these news media. Quite early in the crisis, the *Toronto Star* published a long article critical of the response of the Ford government, which had planned a $13-million cut to Public Health Ontario.[75] It is noticeable that the *Irish Times* was the first to persistently raise questions about how fiscal policies (government emergency spending) are to be paid for.[76]

On the right of the journalist field are Fox News and Breitbart. As described by Benkler in *Network Propaganda* (2018) these media operated outside professional norms of journalism and do not hold themselves responsible to the field of mainstream media. Fox News and Breitbart tended to downplay the importance of Covid-19 (following the example of President Trump) and to lead with negative reports on the Biden presidential campaign. On 22 March 2020, Fox News said: 'As news of the virus spread and death tolls began to spike, many have begun to question how dangerous the new outbreak is.' Fox News blamed the Pandemic on China and supported President Trump when he froze funding to the World Health

Organization. This move by Trump in April 2020 was widely condemned in the mainstream news media. On 24 April 2020, Breitbart led with the headline: 'GOP Rep. Byrne: Media Have Been "Irresponsible" on Coronavirus — "They've Made False Claims, They've Quoted False Statistics"'.

Figure 4: Fox News isolates itself from the norms of professional journalism

New media such as VICE News published occasional scoops but lacked the resources for systematic reporting on the emergency. Both VICE News and BuzzFeed suffered staff cuts during the lockdown. In May 2020, VICE announced lay-offs of 155 workers (about 5 per cent of workers). VICE did publish an article about a leaked Amazon plan to smear striking workers (2 April 2020); and a Kroger employee who said, 'They Call Me a Hero Because I Work at Kroger, So Why Do I Feel Disposable?' (15 May 2020). VICE News also published reports on increased racism towards Asian Americans.[77]

The *Pensacola News Journal*, once a vibrant daily newspaper, mainly reprinted reports from the USA Today network, with only spot news reports about local aspects of the pandemic such as numbers of cases reported, an outbreak in a nursing home and the behaviour of young people on local beaches. This seems to be an example of a community that is poorly served by its local newspaper. By early May 2020, the *Pensacola News Journal* headlines moved on to other stories including forest fires in the area.

Figure 5: Diagram of the field of news media

**ORGANIZATIONS
WITH DEEP RESOURCES**

The Guardian   <<<   New York Times
New Yorker
New Left Review

**QUESTIONS
STATUS QUO**

                   Globe and Mail
                   Toronto Star
                   Irish Times

                                **CONSERVATIVE
POLITICS**

VICE News   Pensacola News Journal   FOX News
                                            Breitbart

Chapter 5

Humans and Animals: One World

What does meat have to do with Covid-19? Meat protein is actually an important aspect of the story: from internet memes that the pandemic was caused by people eating bats, to reports about 'wet markets' in China, where live birds are offered for sale, to governments declaring meat factories an essential service, and slaughter-house workers protesting about unsafe working conditions in the pandemic. How the news media covered these issues is therefore a good test of the news and a useful check on the findings presented in the previous chapter.[78]

Following the pattern described in other chapters of this book there are substantial reports on this issue in magazines such as *The New York Review of Books* and *Wired*. These long reads by writers with real expertise describe industrial food production systems dominated by a small number of large corporations. They describe the systemic exploitation of underpaid labour, often racialized minorities and undocumented migrant workers in the United States. Meat and chicken processing plants operate at a frantic pace, which would have to be slowed down to protect workers from Covid-19. The foods produced by these corporate giants, often with hidden government subsidies and government promotion (for example, of beef consumption), contribute to the unhealthy Western diet. This diet of meat and processed foods makes Americans more vulnerable to health problems such as obesity and diabetes, risk factors for serious outcomes from Covid-19.[79]

A major theme of Mike Davis in *The Monster at Our Doors* (2005) is the relationship between animals and human beings. More than a hundred bat species carry coronaviruses. Typically they don't harm their hosts. The problem arises when these bats interact with small carnivorous animals. Sometimes they are driven together by habitat loss caused by irresponsible development. The diseased animal may be trapped by humans who can then be infected with the virus. Davis also describes viral infections in free-range poultry in Thailand, which probably crossed over from domestic ducks. In 2004, more than 120 million chickens and ducks in Thailand and Vietnam were destroyed in a massive attempt to stop the H5N1 virus from infecting humans.

In the Covid-19 pandemic experts started to notice the reverse: animals are being exposed to the virus by infected human beings. This could be a person taking care of animals or a tourist visiting a National Park. The prospect of the virus circulating among forest animals in the coming years is worrying because quite different variants of the virus could emerge which are resistant to the vaccines now being developed.[80]

Urban poverty is part of the story. Poor people in the Global South often relied on fish protein but factory fishing ships have depleted the stocks. People then turn to other sources of protein such as bushmeat, which is more easily captured due to deforestation. As income levels rise in China, local populations eat more meat and less rice and vegetables. One affordable source of protein is poultry and this normally means factory-farmed chickens. The leader in industrialized poultry and livestock farming is Tyson Foods (Davis, 2020, p. 103). Avian flu can spread like wildfire through these huge operations. There have been frightening outbreaks at chicken factory-farms in Holland, Belgium, Germany and Southern California.

During the Covid-19 pandemic, President Trump ordered meat-processing plants in the United States to remain open to maintain a supply of chicken and meat. *The Guardian* published several articles about this, including a major story about work conditions.[81] As part of its Animals Farmed reporting (supported by the Open Philanthropy Project), *The Guardian* published a report on Covid-19 in meat plants around the world. In Ireland there were outbreaks at ten plants and more than 560 workers affected.[82] *The Guardian* published a separate report about meat plant workers in Ireland, many of whom are migrants and reported unsafe and horrible working conditions in the factories.[83]

In the *Irish Times* there was only a brief report of 560 Covid-19 cases at meat-processing plants in early May 2020.[84] This was followed a few days later by a report that a dozen facilities and up to 600 workers were affected by the disease.[85] But this was not followed up by serious investigative reporting. The issue was really only taken up by the *Irish Times* in July when migrant and workers' organizations gave testimony to a committee of the Irish parliament.[86]

The *New York Times* gave extensive coverage to the issue. A long report by Anna Swanson and others describes workers standing elbow to elbow with only improvised masks at a giant Tyson Foods pork-processing plant in Iowa. Local officials lobbied Tyson to close down the plant but management refused to co-operate. It soon had to close because one-third of the workforce was sick. Then President Trump declared meat-processing plants to be essential and the plant reopened with some safety measures added. Tyson also lobbied the government for protection from lawsuits brought by workers. Many of the workers are migrants and uncertain about their rights. Even with union representation, immigrants at the plant say they are afraid to raise concerns about working conditions.[87]

In Canada, there was extensive coverage in the *Globe and Mail*. A report by Carrie Tait and others described how Cargill Ltd is suspending operations at its meat-packing plant near Montreal after more than 10 per cent of its workforce tested positive for Covid-19. Another plant in Alberta had been shut down when half of the 2000 employees tested positive for the virus. Employees there, often immigrants and temporary foreign workers, say they felt pressured to continue working. This is in spite of having trade-union representation from United Food and Commercial Workers. The workers received some payment for the period when the plant was shut down.[88]

The plight of workers in meat-packing plants is important. But news media rarely expands this topic to deal with the factory farming of chickens, pigs and cattle. This kind of factory farming is related to increased standards of living, associated with meat consumption. In spite of efforts by animal rights activists (criminalized in many parts of the United States) and some interest in vegan diets, the consumption of industrialized meat is widely considered to be normal. President Trump declared meat-processing plants to be an essential service; reducing the supply of meat would have been highly unpopular with his followers. The fact that factory farms are vulnerable to virus infections is mostly off the agenda. The wider perspective that sees factory farms as part of reckless industrial capitalism, and implicated in climate warming, is beyond the sphere of normal news reporting.

Chapter 6

Changes in the News Industry

The Covid-19 pandemic placed huge demands on news media. Part of the problem was that traditional news organizations were already in a weakened position. Deregulation of the media in the 1980s resulted in the sale of many local newspapers to conglomerates or speculative investors. Newspapers burdened by debt had to lay off reporters, resulting in a less interesting paper, often with little coverage of local news. The dependence of North American papers on advertising revenue left them vulnerable to advertising sites such as Craig's List and to social media which soon attracted buckets of advertising dollars.

A report for the Pew Research Center found that Americans who primarily get news through social media are least informed about Covid-19.[89] The Reuters Institute *Digital News Report* shows that there are substantial increases in the consumption of news during the pandemic.[90] Television news saw a considerable uptick, in part because of distribution problems of printed newspapers. The use of online and social media substantially increased. Trust in the mainstream media coverage of Covid-19 was high, twice the level of trust in social media. During the pandemic, people turned to traditional media for news.

Although people are turning to news media for information about the pandemic, advertising income has plummeted because economic activity has been drastically curtailed. The *New York Times* estimated that 37,000 workers at news companies have been affected in the United States (including temporary lay-offs and pay cuts). Those affected include 13 employees (4 journalists) laid off at the *Denver Post*, 31 lay-offs at *Sports Illustrated*, and a 4-day workweek at VICE, with pay cuts of 10 per cent or 20 per cent.[91] *The Guardian* soon reported that BuzzFeed has closed its UK and Australian news operations.[92] The *Toronto Star* announced on April 6 that it planned to eliminate 85 positions and reduce executive pay. In late May 2020, the *Toronto Star* was purchased by an investment company for $52 million.[93]

Another study by the Pew Research Center found that advertising revenue fell 42 per cent for American newspapers in the second quarter of 2020 by comparison with the previous year. Many newspapers responded by laying off employees. However, ad revenue for television network news rose 11 per cent and jumped 41 per cent for Fox News Channel. Audiences turned to TV in record numbers for news about the pandemic.[94]

News sources

Since this is a medical emergency, news organizations turn to experts for information and analysis. But who is permitted to speak?

Political leaders are given a platform which is greater than in normal times. Daily press conferences by the Prime Minister of Canada and the Ontario premier are widely covered by the media. These are public-relations events, with carefully written scripts. Reporters have an opportunity to ask questions but these are normally restricted in scope: they are often simply requests for additional information. What media are permitted to participate? Which journalists are allowed to ask questions? A crisis such as the coronavirus pandemic may result in a legitimacy crisis (Was the government prepared? Did it take the virus threat seriously?) and these press conferences are exercises in political power. Before the crisis the Premier of Ontario was quite unpopular due to cutbacks to education and other public services.

Local medical experts are interviewed. These are often doctors working in large urban hospitals, or specialists in infectious diseases and epidemiology. Although epidemiology deals with social aspects of disease, these experts are mainly asked questions about the spread of the virus and whether it is being controlled. How are these experts chosen by news organizations? In fact, many of them were quite critical of government responses, the lack of testing and the speed with which the economy was opened up after closures that lasted from 8 to 10 weeks. Another journalist can also be treated as an expert, for example Andre Picard, health reporter for the *Globe and Mail*, author of several books on public health in Canada (and also critical of the speed with which the Ontario economy was opened up).[95]

The news media turns to medical experts, even on issues where there are other bodies of research and expertise. For example, doctors speak about schools but sociologists of education are ignored. Doctors talk about mobile-phone apps with no special expertise on issues of privacy and surveillance capitalism.

Most media invited a wide range of medical experts (this was noticeable on CBC Radio news) and they did not always say the same thing.[96] Reporters are generally silent about divergences of opinion among doctors and various experts. On 28 January 2021, the CBC 1 radio call-in show *Ontario Today* has a doctor from the Ontario expert group advising the government, who makes excuses for the second wave of deaths in long-term residences: there are many factors, staff are exhausted, there are challenges that need to be addressed after the pandemic.[97] Why did the CBC not invite Doctors for Justice in LTC which just issued a quite different statement on this issue?[98]

A year into the pandemic, Dr Michael Warner spoke out against the Ford government which he said is mostly guided by unnamed medical experts. The Premier of Ontario has taken no action on paid sick leave or paid leave to get vaccinated. The age-based guidelines are no longer appropriate in the third wave, with variants of the virus. Vaccines should be redirected to communities where infection is greatest. Mobile teams should bring the vaccines to factories and warehouses. At his hospital, he is seeing mostly people who cannot protect themselves from the virus because of the work they do. These are most often low-paid racialized workers (CBC *Metro Morning*, 31 March 2021).

In Ontario, the government repeatedly said it was following medical advice. It relied heavily on a conservative medical adviser. The news media in general did not question this, or examine in detail policy decisions apparently taken while following medical advice. A broader range of medical voices was gradually heard in the news. In the crisis of the third wave, in Spring 2021, Dr Peter Juni started to speak out and make statements that criticized government policies, especially the situation of unpaid sick leave, but also the failure to prioritize at-risk neighbourhoods and workers in factories, warehouses and meat-packing plants. But for months, this kind of critical voice was not heard in the news.

World medical experts appear less often in news media. The press seemed not to turn to the World Health Organization, though the chief executive director of the WHO Health Emergencies Programme, Dr Mike Ryan, is sometimes quoted. Is this because of the lack of availability of WHO speakers? Or a delegitimization of the World Health Organization? *The Guardian* has the most articles based on WHO sources, including Dr Ryan (as it happens) speaking out against contact-tracing apps on privacy grounds.

Critical social scientists are mostly excluded from mainstream media. Mike Davis, the author of *The Monster at Our Door* (2005), appears in alternative media such as the Jacobin Magazine YouTube channel, but his complex analysis of dangerous viruses, ecological change, industrial development, commercial agriculture and factory farms seemed beyond the media frame of a pandemic created by a virus. Certainly, many more people were exposed to President Trump's speculations about a virus that escaped from a Chinese research laboratory than the complex analysis of social scientists.[99]

Differences in the news audience

This book has emphasized that serious investigative reporting about Covid-19 is available for readers who seek it out. However, these long reads are sometimes hidden behind paywalls and require effort to find. These items are not the short, dramatic or conflictual items that tend to circulate on social media. Johan Lindell's research in Sweden shows that there are different audience segments for digital news. The business sector is generally well-informed about current events and reads the online editions of financial newspapers. The liberal professions, artists and cultural workers are also well-informed and tend to read more liberal online newspapers, similar to *The Guardian*. The traditional working class is less informed and more likely to be suspicious of journalists (in the United States they may follow Fox News). Young people and students are also less informed, more interested in celebrity and sports news on social media.[100]

Figure 6: Most commented and most shared items for the *Guardian*, April 9, 2020.

Most viewed		
1	●Live / Coronavirus live news: Iran deaths pass 4,000 as US insists isolation measures are working after record daily toll	6 UK coronavirus lockdown 'to be extended beyond next week'
2	Have Australia and New Zealand stopped Covid-19 in its tracks?	7 Coronavirus map of the US: latest cases state by state
3	How did coronavirus start and where did it come from? Was it really Wuhan's animal market?	8 How coronavirus spread across the globe - visualised
4	Lockdowns can't end until Covid-19 vaccine found, study says	9 Global coronavirus cases near 1.5m as fresh WHO row erupts
5	The cluster effect: how social gatherings were rocket fuel for coronavirus	10 Coronavirus UK: how many confirmed cases are in your area?

Most commented
Corbyn has gone, but Keir Starmer's Labour still depends on the grassroots left
Jack Shenker

Most shared
NHS staff forbidden from speaking out publicly about coronavirus

It is possible to find good investigative reporting on Covid-19. But these reports and expert opinion pieces are usually not the most-read items online. We might even say that the distinguishing feature of quality mainstream journalism today is to commission in-depth and thoughtful writing, supported by fact-checking, and to publish it even though it is not what most people are reading. Investigative articles and long reads will mainly reach middle-class audiences with higher levels of education.

News frames and media narratives

Media researchers talk about a news frame or narrative. News is not simply the presentation of facts. It organizes information into coherent stories. Of necessity, these narratives work to suppress other alternative frames or narratives. These oppositional ways of telling the story can sometimes be found in alternative sources (magazines such as the *New Yorker*, or *New Left Review*) which seldom circulate on social media. They are often hidden behind paywalls.

Other researchers speak of the role of political elites in setting news agendas: directing our attention in one direction and not another. One of the most frequent words uttered by the Prime Minister of Canada about the pandemic is 'unprecedented'. The Premier of Ontario puts it in more populist language when he says repeatedly that nobody could have seen this coming.

This kind of frame has the effect of bumping other perspectives and issues off the news agenda. For example, no news organization in Ontario reported that as late as 4 March 2020 the government of Ontario was fighting with the Ontario Nurses' Association, forcing nurses to accept a 1-percent pay increase.[101] Governments around the world adopted military metaphors about 'frontline workers'. This diverts attention from the unions that represent at least some of these workers. The Ontario Nurses' Association took the government of

Ontario to court in an attempt to get it to listen. Union leaders representing personal support workers did not get much of a hearing (CBC Radio was the occasional exception here). *The Guardian* published a piece by an anonymous doctor saying that they do not want people clapping for them because it diverts attention from decades of government cutbacks and this is where the emphasis should be put.[102]

In the initial period of the crisis, the Canadian media never refutes this frame: the pandemic is unprecedented. We are living in unprecedented times. The media allows politicians to frame the issues in this way and never challenges this myth. And so if governments are unprepared, or fail to take action in the Summer of 2020 (before the second wave), or just make mistakes, or absurd claims (work on condo building sites in Ontario should continue through the lockdown because housing is an essential service), it can be forgiven because this is all without precedent.[103]

This media myth is extraordinary because Toronto did have a precedent in 2003 with the SARS outbreak. And the official reports produced about SARS included warnings about a possible repeat, with a similar virus, sometime in the future. Ontario was warned to be prepared.[104]

Chapter 7

The Stories That Are Not Told

There are three fundamental stories that were never told. Someone with a lot of time and good research skills could discover them. But they were never repeated with enough force and clarity to break through the dominant emphasis on case numbers, the availability of vaccines, or internet memes about bat soup or Vitamin C. These stories are:

1. The delay in taking the virus seriously in China, but also in the rest of the world;
2. A failure to register the seriousness of the crisis and its causes (similar to the failure to respond to the climate crisis);
3. A lack of investigative reporting into the details of economic policies taken in response to the pandemic.

The first story has been told for the response in China. In the initial outbreak, authorities in Wuhan tried to cover up the outbreak and control the media.[105] Dr Li Wenliang tried to raise the alarm but was censored, and subsequently died from Covid-19. However, when Beijing took over from local authorities, all of this changed. Public health measures were rapidly imposed, medical services ramped up, and the genetic map of the virus was identified and communicated to medical experts around the world. There are moving accounts of what people in Wuhan experienced.[106]

However, a very similar delay in the West has mostly been ignored. If we look back at the first news reports we find items such as Sarah Boseley, 'China's Sars-like illness worries health experts', *The Guardian*, 9 January 2020, and Rob Wallace, 'Notes on a novel coronavirus', MR Online, 29 January 2020. Boseley's report is tentative but concludes that a cluster of patients with an unusual respiratory disease should be taken seriously. Rob Wallace is an expert in environment and disease. He issued a stark warning: 'Chinese authorities have reported 5974 cases nationwide, 1000 of them severe. With infections in nearly every province, authorities warned 2019-nCoV appears to be spreading fast out of its epicenter.' The virus seems to be a serious global threat. His article is written in a tone of despair, because political leaders do not take this risk seriously.[107] Research shows that there were over 3000 news reports about the outbreak published before 20 January 2020, the date on which the Chinese government made an official announcement.[108] It seems that the world was not paying attention.

The emergency unfolded differently around the world. In Ontario, where I live, no real action was taken until 12 March 2020. That is a delay of 6 or 8 weeks. Taking action during this time could have had enormous consequences. Cases of the disease might already have arrived in Canada, carried by tourists and business people, but contact tracing of people who got sick might have limited the spread of the disease. Why did this not happen? Inertia perhaps? People absorbed in running a business or a university look to the ordinary schedule of activities: a business meeting, a marketing event. A respiratory disease in China does not register. The sociologist Pierre Bourdieu talks about a *habitus*, a structure of experience. We worry about tomorrow's business meeting, or ordering coffee for a marketing event. Our taken for granted experience is immediate and pressing. Talk about a pandemic seems remote and unreal. One university administrator said to me: nothing is going to happen here.

In a more radical perspective, we might think about structures of capitalism, which Raymond Williams describes as setting limits to what seems possible and exerting pressures that make any alternative seem unlikely.[109] Think of capitalism as a train, running on schedule in a direction already laid out in the train tracks. A powerful engine pulls us along, we are the passengers. To stop this train, or have it move in a different direction, seems completely impossible. When someone gives an emergency signal, few people pay attention to the whistle-blower.

The second untold story has to do with the seriousness of the Covid-19 pandemic. It is now clear that mainstream media did not absorb the seriousness of the disease. After the initial shock, the temporal frame was that it would all be over in a few months. The idea of a second wave and a third wave did not register even though experts were aware that a more serious second wave was likely. There was little discussion of variants of the virus, though this is a basic scientific fact: this kind of virus makes copies that change and evolve. Changes that give an advantage to the virus, as it tries to make a living, are favoured and likely to be more dangerous to human hosts. This is well-known by virologists. But this narrative did not register with sufficient force in mainstream news media.

The media did not register that Covid-19 is a wake-up call, similar in gravity to the environmental crisis, to which it is actually linked.[110] The memes about an 'unprecedented crisis', military metaphors such as 'frontline workers' and disbelief in the reality of Covid-19 function to distract attention from the fundamental seriousness of the pandemic. In the first months there was little reporting about the possibility of a second wave of infections, in spite of the fact that the second wave of the 1918 pandemic was more serious than the original wave. The virus was generally imagined as a foreign agent or bug that could be contained. There was little discussion about RNA-based viruses that invade animal or human cells to replicate themselves, described by Mike Davis as a manic Xerox machine that keeps making errors. Experts knew this, of course. But it did not register with the public that variants of SARS-CoV-2 might emerge that were more transmissible and more deadly.

Quality newspapers give some space to the Covid-19 pandemic in international news. There are dramatic stories about deaths in Brazil and heartless measures in India that forced migrant workers to trek back to their rural homes. Occasionally there is mention of a medical crisis in Ecuador or Mexico. Africa is dealt with a broad brush and apparently will have to wait for vaccines. Palestinians will go unvaccinated, while Israel leads in vaccinating its own citizens. There is little overall sense of the gravity of the global situation. How will life in the USA or Europe return to normal with dangerous variants of the virus circulating in the Global South? How does this fit with the original hope, amplified in news media, that this crisis might be over in a few months? Should we not have recognized that we will be living with this crisis for many years?[111]

The pandemic exposes, if the story could be told, all that is wrong about the irresponsible path of industrial capitalism.[112] Reckless environmental destruction is almost certainly responsible for the virus jumping from an animal host to human beings. And there are hundreds of similar viruses to monitor and worry about. (This is one of the roles of the World Health Organization and why it needs to be funded to adequately monitor viruses that may become future threats.) The virus travels rapidly along the trade routes that manufactured goods from China take to the rest of the world, or the virus hops aboard the next available flight, carried along by global tourists and business executives.

Voices that spoke about the seriousness of this pandemic, and a future more devastating disease, were generally not heard. In spite of his participation in the movie *Contagion* (2011), which proved to be a surprisingly accurate portrayal of the Covid-19 pandemic, Larry Brilliant's message about public health was not amplified in the news media. Brilliant argues that the virus will be around for some time, especially in the developing world where new variants will emerge. He points out that the collective measures for global security put in place following the Second World War have been eroded since the 1980s by a turn to neoliberalism and the argument that the free market works best. Government-funded public health measures that are needed to contain serious diseases have been cut back over the past 30 years.[113]

In Canada, we have seen that the virus exposes all that is wrong about our society: systemic inequality and systemic racism, gender inequalities, cutbacks to public services and health services done in the name of market capitalism ('saving taxpayers' money'), inequality in access to the internet, the education to make use of online resources and make judgements about information and opinions found online. The deregulation of the media industries from the 1980s weakened our news organizations and made them vulnerable to the ninja blow from social media corporations.

The third untold story is related to this. One month into the crisis in North America, it was quite difficult to find good analyses of the macroeconomic effects of the pandemic and the full details of government fiscal and monetary policies. The media reports fiscal policies such as payments to unemployed workers and small businesses but there is much less attention to monetary policies and the prospects for the near future (the coming 2 years).[114]

Many reports on the economic effects of the pandemic describe the contraction of businesses, from corner barber shops to large construction projects temporarily closed. The International Monetary Fund predicted that economic growth in the United States would fall by 5.9 per cent. There were reports that the Chinese economy contracted by 6.8 per cent. Unemployment rates would be worse than during the Depression of the 1930s. Debate in news media was about when to 'open up' the economy.[115] By late April there was some reporting of conservative politicians opposed to increased government spending. The *Irish Times* warned that difficult choices would have to be made. The *Globe and Mail* was more optimistic.[116] *The Guardian* published Opinion pieces arguing for continued government spending and a fairer tax system.[117]

Economists warned about the possibility of government borrowing increasing inflation which would in turn result in Central Banks increasing interest rates and therefore the cost of governments' borrowing. A very careful reader might have come across explanations of quantitative easing of the money supply by Central Banks, the same strategy used for the global financial crisis of 2007-08.[118]

It is still difficult to find analysis that goes beyond description of the economic effects of the pandemic. Adam Tooze, author of *Crashed: How a Decade of Financial Crisis Changed the World*, published a long piece in *The Guardian* about how coronavirus almost brought down the global financial system, but it seems mainly a description of how central banks (not elected politicians) acted to prevent disaster.[119] Joseph Stiglitz describes the lack of funding for public goods in the United States, but his main suggestion is more funding for research.[120] It took Robert Brenner (and his research assistant) to comb the media for reports apparently showing massive state support to large corporations. It would take a very careful reader of half a dozen elite newspapers to put this picture together.[121]

It is not the purpose of this book to add to the widespread suspicion of mainstream media. The meme that 'it is all lies' simply enables powerful actors and corporations that would much rather control decisions with as little opposition as possible. The cynical attitude that all news is fake news only benefits those in power who wish to avoid publicity about what they are doing. This book has shown that mainstream news media (excluding Fox News) did a good job in educating the public on the basic facts about the coronavirus. At times, the mainstream media went beyond this to ask tough questions and address the systemic underlying issues thrown up by the pandemic emergency. It is true that these long reads are mainly accessible to educated middle-class readers. The solution is not to attack these reports for their 'elitism' but to work for a long revolution in culture and education that make serious journalism available for the majority of the world's citizens.[122]

Writing about the economic consequences of the pandemic, Grace Blakeley offers an analysis of the relation between state and capitalism that is far from the neoliberal myth of a free market system.[123] Blakeley describes the relation between governments and large corporations as state monopoly capitalism. In this system, decisions about which enterprises will succeed and which will be allowed to fail are taken by elites and not by the market system. Airplane construction will be rescued (supposedly vital to national security), industrialized farming of animals will be subsidized, emergency research on vaccines will be funded by the government but the drug companies allowed to profit from them, the oil industry will be heavily promoted, even though its environmental effects are well understood.[124] Many small businesses will be permitted to fail (increasing the alienation of this sector of society) and many people will lose their jobs.[125] Newspapers will be allowed to fall into bankruptcy, while the frightening power of a handful of social media corporations mostly goes unchecked. Looking around the United States in the 1940s, the German refugees Adorno and Horkheimer detected a similar system of state capitalism.[126] They called it a system of economic rackets. Aware of the role of the media and the culture industry, they speculated about its role in such a system. How can this system of economic 'rackets' be legitimated to citizens? Adorno gave his own prediction: a media industry that distracts attention from what is happening; mass culture that promotes either total conformity or the irresponsible attitude of the complete outsider. If this nightmare world were ever established, all news would be 'fake news'.

Appendix 1

Sample of Canadian Broadcasting Corporation Coverage of Covid-19

CBC News Covid-19 March 2020 (top results on Google)
https://www.cbc.ca/player/play/1712932419885
https://www.cbc.ca/player/play/1711952963750
https://www.cbc.ca/player/play/1715366979734
https://www.cbc.ca/player/play/1714808387606
https://www.cbc.ca/kidsnews/post/here-are-the-latest-facts-about-the-coronavirus
https://www.cbc.ca/player/play/1847307843822
https://www.cbc.ca/news/canada/ottawa/covid19-coronavirus-ottawa-symptoms-information-march-27-1.5511735
https://www.youtube.com/watch?v=YhUn1IY97-4
https://www.cbc.ca/news/canada/coronavirus-covid19-canada-world-may10-1.5563513
https://www.cbc.ca/player/play/1710416963669

CBC News Covid-19 April 2020 (top results on Google)
https://www.cbc.ca/news/canada/coronavirus-covid19-1.5545450
https://www.cbc.ca/news/canada/coronavirus-covid19-april3-canada-world-1.5519144
https://www.cbc.ca/news/canada/coronavirus-covid19-april21-canada-world-1.5538530
https://www.cbc.ca/news/canada/nova-scotia/nova-scotia-covid-19-update-sunday-april-19-1.5537729
https://www.cbc.ca/player/play/1726225987698
https://www.cbc.ca/news/canada/nova-scotia/nova-scotia-covid-19-27-new-cases-total-606-1.5535823
https://www.cbc.ca/player/play/1719196227752

https://www.cbc.ca/news/canada/newfoundland-labrador/
covid19-newfoundland-labrador-april-24-1.5543852

CBC News Covid-19 May 2020 (top results on Google)
https://www.cbc.ca/news/canada/coronavirus-covid19-canada-
world-may10-1.5563513
https://www.cbc.ca/news/canada/coronavirus-covid19-canada-
may24-sunday-1.5582365
https://www.cbc.ca/news/canada/coronavirus-covid19-canada-
world-may9-1.5562989
https://www.cbc.ca/player/play/1839184963612
https://www.cbc.ca/news/canada/coronavirus-covid19-canada-
may14-1.5569147
https://www.cbc.ca/news/canada/ottawa/covid19-coronavirus-
ottawa-symptoms-information-may-29-1.5589515
https://www.cbc.ca/news/canada/newfoundland-labrador/
covid19-newfoundland-labrador-may-6-1.5557543
https://www.cbc.ca/news/canada/ottawa/covid19-coronavirus-
ottawa-symptoms-information-may-20-1.5576205
https://www.cbc.ca/news/canada/ottawa/covid19-coronavirus-
ottawa-symptoms-information-may-22-1.5579743
https://www.cbc.ca/news/canada/nova-scotia/nova-scotia-
covid-19-update-tuesday-may-26-1.5585053

Examples of News Reports about Fundamental Aspects of Covid-19

Fundamental assessments of the crisis appeared in the news media by May 2020. See for example, Robin McKie and others, 100 days later: How did Britain fail so badly in dealing with Covid-19? *The Guardian*, 10 May 2020. This Sunday edition of *The Guardian* provides a wide-ranging assessment of how the pandemic exposes fundamental issues of social inequality and the effects of decades of neoliberal policies. See also, Nesrine Malik, There is revolution in the air now, but history shows the old order will fight back, *The Guardian*, 18 May 2020.

Medical experts and social scientists warn about a pandemic

David Quammen, Why Weren't We Ready for the Coronavirus? *New Yorker*, 4 May 2020.

Jennifer Kahn, How Scientists Could Stop the Next Pandemic Before It Starts, *New York Times Magazine*, 21 April 2020.

Mike Davis, The Monster Enters, *New Left Review*, March-April 2020.

Social determinants of health

Anne Case and Angus Deaton, America Can Afford a World-Class Health System: Why Don't We Have One? (Opinion), *New York Times*, 14 April 2020.

Lauren Aratani and Dominic Rushe, African Americans bear the brunt of Covid-19's economic impact, *The Guardian*, 28 April 2020.

Jennifer Yang and others, Toronto's Covid-19 divide: The city's northwest corner has been 'failed by the system', *Toronto Star*, 28 June 2020.

Pandemic in the Global South
Caio Barretto Briso and Tom Phillips, Rio's favelas count the cost as deadly spread of Covid-19 hits city's poor, *The Guardian*, 25 April 2020.

Ioan Grillo, The Specter of Mexico's Coronavirus Crash, *New York Times*, 29 April 2020.

N. R. Musahar, India's Starvation Measures, *New Left Review*, March-April 2020.

BBC *Business Daily*, How can Africa emerge from lockdown? 21 April 2020 online at: https://www.bbc.co.uk/sounds/play/w3csz895

Conditions in long-term residences
The Guardian view on the care home crisis: culpable neglect (Editorial), *The Guardian*, 14 April 2020.

Matthew Goldstein and others, Push for Profits Leaves Nursing Homes Struggling to Provide Care During Coronavirus Pandemic, *New York Times*, 7 May 2020.

Richard Mollot, Nursing Homes Were a Disaster Waiting to Happen (Opinion), *New York Times*, 28 April 2020.

Alexandra Villarreal, US nursing homes seek legal immunity as Covid-19 spreads 'like brushfire', *The Guardian*, 13 May 2020.

Tu Thanh Ha, Inspection reports reveal critical gaps inside Quebec nursing homes ravaged by Covid-19, *Globe and Mail*, 26 May 2020.

The digital divide
Shira Ovide, 'We Can Do Better': One Plan to Erase America's Digital Divide, *New York Times*, 14 April 2020.

Shira Ovide, Why Rural America's Digital Divide Persists, *New York Times*, 5 May 2020.

Dana Floberg, US students are being asked to work remotely. But 22 per cent of homes don't have internet, *The Guardian*, 23 March 2020.

Annie Kelly, Digital divide 'isolates and endangers' millions of UK's poorest, *The Guardian*, 28 April 2020.

Tim Berners-Lee, Covid-19 makes it clearer than ever: access to the internet should be a universal right (Opinion), *The Guardian*, 4 June 2020.

Macroeconomic effects of the pandemic

Robert Brenner, Escalating Plunder, *New Left Review*, May-June 2020.

Adam Tooze, How coronavirus almost brought down the global financial system, *The Guardian*, 14 April 2020.

Joseph E. Stiglitz, A Lasting Remedy for the Covid-19 Pandemic's Economic Crisis, New York Review of Books Daily, 8 April 2020.

Appendix 3

The New York Times and Amazon Warehouses

A search of the *New York Times* for 'Amazon and Covid-19' from 15 March to 31 May 2020 gives nine results. The research question is whether these items expand the sphere of legitimate controversy in the *Times*.

The first item is We Need Amazon During the Coronavirus: That's a Problem by Greg Bensinger, a member of the *Times* editorial board (31 March 2020). The Opinion piece argues that Federal assistance has gone to large corporations rather than small retailers such as Powell's Books. Amazon is criticized as a monopoly that abuses its dominant position. Amazon is hiring 100,00 temporary workers but Bensinger criticizes its working conditions and reports that some workers have walked off the job over lack of preventive measures against Covid-19.

There is a news report by Karen Weise and Kate Conger, Gaps in Amazon's Response as Virus Spreads to More Than 50 Warehouses (April 6, 2020). Amazon's mostly non-unionized employees are protesting work conditions and up to 30 percent are not reporting for work in warehouses. A worker involved in these protests was fired. There are Covid-19 outbreaks in 50 of Amazon's 500 warehouses in the United States. The tone of the report is fairly critical of Amazon.

The third piece is in the Technology section. Shira Ovide does an interview about how Amazon is coping with increased demand during the pandemic (22 April 2020). This is completely uncritical of Amazon.

The same day, technology reporter Karen Weise reports that Jeff Bezos is personally involved in Amazon's response to the pandemic, Bezos Takes Back the Wheel at Amazon (22

April 2020). The tone is critical of Bezos's affluent lifestyle. He seems more concerned about shareholders than workers. For the first time in years he actually visits an Amazon warehouse. He ordered face masks for employees but there are problems with delivery. Amazon has been criticized for firing employees who protested work conditions in its warehouses.

A week later, Karen Weise reports that sales by Amazon are up but profits have fallen and Jeff Bezos seems anxious to reassure shareholders: Amazon Sells More, but Warns of Much Higher Costs Ahead (30 April 2020). Amazon had to hire more workers and pay for safety measures. The tone of the article is neutral but it does mention: 'On a call with reporters, the company declined to say how many of its workers had tested positive for the virus.'

The *Times* business reporter Mihir Zaveri takes a much more critical tone when a senior Amazon executive resigns in protest against the firing of workers who organized pickets to highlight dangerous work conditions in warehouses: 'An Amazon Vice President Quit Over Firings of Employees Who Protested' (5 May 2020). Meeting notes leaked to VICE News showed Amazon lawyers attempting to discredit an employee who protested. The executive who quit describes Amazon as an example of twenty-first century capitalism that treats workers badly.

The next item is a report by Liz Alderman and Adam Satariano from Paris: 'Amazon's Showdown in France Tests Its Ability to Sidestep Labor' (14 May 2020). Amazon has resisted the unionization of its workers, but employees in France are unionized. A French court ordered Amazon to stop shipping non-essential items to protect worker health in the pandemic. The *Times* reports that: 'Amazon has not disclosed how many warehouse workers have contracted Covid-19 in Europe, but cases have been reported in France, Germany, Italy, Poland and Spain.'

Karen Weise reports on the largest Covid-19 outbreak at an Amazon warehouse in the United States: 'Way Too Late': Inside Amazon's Biggest Outbreak (19 May 2020). About 100 workers were infected at a warehouse in Pennsylvania, but Amazon refused to give full details. Workers describe lax safety standards.

John Herrman published a long article in the *New York Times Magazine*: 'Amazon's Big Breakdown' (22 May 2020). The article describes Amazon's e-commerce machine failing under pressure from online orders in the first phase of the pandemic. There was a surge in sales but Jeff Bezos was warning shareholders about a drop in profits. Amazon hired more workers and its stock rose in value, increasing Bezos's personal wealth. The article describes how the Amazon platform works in normal times. In the pandemic its treatment of workers seems heavy-handed: 'On March 30, a week after Amazon confirmed its first case to JFK8 workers, an employee named Chris Smalls, citing worker-safety concerns like a lack of protective equipment, led a walkout; about 2 hours after it ended, Smalls was told he had been fired.' Other employees were treated in the same way. 'Amazon is operating in a profoundly friendly regulatory and tax environment; at the National Labor Relations Board, charged with investigating labor complaints, Trump appointees are firmly in control.'

There are two linked articles in which the keyword 'Covid-19' is not used. 'Strikes at Instacart and Amazon Over Coronavirus Health Concerns' by Noam Scheiber and Kate Conger (30 March 2020) describes protests by workers at Instacart and Amazon facilities over safety and inadequate pay. A Vice News article circulated about these protests and workers in other cities joining in (including at Whole Foods and Trader Joe's). The article is balanced by a quote from Amazon but is clearly sympathetic to the workers.

A second article takes an even stronger position in favour

of workers. 'We Didn't Sign Up For This': Amazon Workers on the Front Lines, by Gina Belafante (3 April 2020) describes the expansion of Amazon in the pandemic and says that Amazon has always resisted the efforts of organized labour. The writer interviews Chris Smalls, the employee fired by Amazon for organizing a protest against the corporation's decision not to temporarily close down a New York warehouse with Covid-19 cases.

Endnotes

1   Maria Cramer, Investigating Amazon, the Employer, *New York Times*, 4 July 2021.

2   In June 2021 the *New York Times* has much less coverage of the continuing pandemic than *The Guardian*. It also gives more space to speculations about the release of SARS-CoV-2 from a research lab in China. This results in less attention to other issues in the pandemic and the continuing crisis in many parts of the world. The sphere of legitimate controversy seems to have shrunk from a year ago, and the NYT is once again reflecting the worldview of the ruling elite in the USA.

3   Eszter Hargittai and Alice Marwick, 'What Can I Really Do?' Explaining the Privacy Paradox with Online Apathy, *International Journal of Communication* (2016) 10: 3737–3757; Shaul A. Duke, Nontargets: Understanding the Apathy Towards the Israeli Security Agency's COVID-19 Surveillance, *Surveillance & Society* (2021) 19,1: 114-129; Johan Lindell and Paola Sartoretto, Young People, Class and the News: Distinction, socialization and moral sentiments, *Journalism Studies* (2018) 19,14: 2042-2061.

4   By the end of May 2020 the media is full of reports of lockdowns lifted, economies reopened and protests in the USA against a 'fake' pandemic. Experts worried about a second wave caused by all this. David Hunter, The coronavirus infection rate is still too high: There will probably be a second wave, *The Guardian*, 28 May 2020.

5   Damian Carrington, Climate crisis: 2020 was joint hottest year ever recorded, *The Guardian*, 8 January 2021.

6   The original report can be consulted on the Internet Archive website at https://archive.org/details/Lippmann MerzATestoftheNews

7   W. Lance Bennett, Toward a Theory of Press-State Relations in the United States, *Journal of Communication* (1990) offers a similar analysis.

8   It is important to understand the conditions that make autonomous journalism possible. Sometimes this is a newspaper protected from market forces by a trust fund. There are examples of quality magazines funded by high-priced advertising directed at elite readers. In some cases a daily newspaper may have a tradition of supporting working-class and liberal politics.

9   Benkler's argument does not rely on psychological theories of conservative personality traits (pp. 335-6).

10   Amy Mitchell and others, Americans Who Mainly Get Their News on Social Media Are Less Engaged, Less Knowledgeable. Pew Research Centre, July 2020. Jon Roozenbeek and others, Susceptibility to misinformation about COVID-19 around the world, *Royal Society Open Science* (2020), 7.

11   Kathleen Hall Jamieson and Dolores Albarracin, The Relation between Media Consumption and Misinformation at the Outset of the SARS-Cov-2 Pandemic in the US. *Harvard Kennedy School Misinformation Review*, April 2020.

12   Aengus Bridgeman and others, The causes and consequences of Covid-19 misperceptions: Understanding the role of news and social media. *Harvard Kennedy School Misinformation Review*, April 2020. See also Matt Motta and others, How Right-Leaning Media Coverage of COVID-19 Facilitated the Spread of Misinformation in the Early Stages of the Pandemic in the US, *Canadian Journal of Political Science* (2020), 53, 335-342.

13   Guy Bessette, *Involving the Community: A Guide to Participatory Development Communication*. Ottawa: IDRC, 2004.

14   Robert Faris and others, *Polarization and the Pandemic:*

American Political Discourse March-May 2020. Berkman Klein Center for Internet & Society Research, October 2020. This study reports that in the middle of March the focus of media attention was almost entirely on Covid-19. The proportion of media attention to the pandemic diminished in April and May. The study also finds that larger traditional media organizations, with more resources and staff, generally perform better in covering the crisis.

15   Yochai Benkler, Robert Faris and Hal Roberts, *Network Propaganda: Manipulation, Disinformation, and Radicalization in American Politics.* New York: Oxford University Press, 2018.

16   Laurie Garrett, Trump Has Sabotaged America's Coronavirus Response, *Foreign Policy* 31 January 2020.

17   A study of coverage of Covid-19 on the three major US television networks (excluding Fox) and six major newspapers found that in the period from March to May 2020 politicians' responses to the pandemic were different for Democrats and Republicans. In the early period of the pandemic, politicians were more frequently mentioned in the news than scientists. P Sol Hart, Sedona Chinn and Stuart Soroka, Politicization and Polarization in Covid-19 News Coverage, *Science Communication* (2020), 42: 6799-697.

18   Wasim Ahmed and others, Covid-19 and the G5 Conspiracy Theory: Social Network Analysis of Twitter Data, *Journal of Medical Internet Research* (2020) 22,5.

19   *The House*, CBC Radio, Saturday 11 April 2020.

20   Katie Pedersen, Melissa Mancini and David Common, Ontario scaled back comprehensive, annual inspections of nursing homes to only a handful last year, https://www.cbc.ca/news/canada/seniors-home-inspections-1.5532585 For praise of Ford see Heather Mallick, Ontario Premier Doug Ford has flipped my world, *Toronto Star*, 18 May

2020, and Marie Henein, My uncomfortable reality: Doug Ford is the leader Ontario needs, *Globe and Mail*, 9 May 2020.

21 This search was done on 17 February 2021, in Toronto on the Google website and using a computer that normally does not use Google Search. Search is for VIDEOS using the keywords: CBC News Covid-19 and the month in 2020. The results include a CBC webpage for children and one radio programme. For some reason the top results for May 2020 include Dr Bonnie Henry's end-of-year message on CBC.

22 For an example of a more critical approach a year later see, The National, How delays in acknowledging airborne Covid-19 transmission risked lives, CBC Television, 16 June 2021, https://www.cbc.ca/player/play/1910139971514

23 The *Sunday Edition* for 19 April 2020 with host Michael Enright includes a discussion of surveillance and invasions of privacy in the pandemic, with Brenda McPhail from the Canadian Civil Liberties Association.

24 Debra E Blakely, Social Construction of Three Influenza Pandemics in the *New York Times*, *Journalism & Mass Communication Quarterly* (2003) 80,4: 884-902, examines how the media frame changes from the 1918 flu pandemic, to the Asian flu pandemic of 1957 and the Hong Kong flu in 1968.

25 Peter LM Vasterman and Nel Ruigrok, Pandemic alarm in the Dutch media: Media coverage of the 2009 influenza H1N1 pandemic and the role of experts, *European Journal of Communication* 28(4): 436-453.

26 Seow Ting Lee and Iccha Basnyat, From Press Release to News: Mapping the Framing of the 20009 H1N1 A Influenza Pandemic, *Health Communication* (2013), 28. See also, Irina Milutinovic, Media framing of Covid-19 pandemic in the transitional regime of Serbia: Exploring discourses and

strategies, *Media, Culture & Society* (2021), which finds that in authoritarian Serbia there is little investigative or critical journalism about Covid-19.

27   Corey H. Basch, Aleksander Kecojic and Victoria H. Wagner, Coverage of the Covid-19 Pandemic in Online Versions of Highly Circulated US Daily Newspapers, *Journal of Community Health* (2020), 45: 1089-1097.

28   Robert Farris and others, *Polarization and the Pandemic: American Political Discourse, March-May 2020.* Berkman Klein Center, 2020. Daniel Romer and Kathleen Hall Jamieson, Patterns of Media Use, Strength of Belief in Covid-19 Conspiracy Theories, *Journal of Medical Internet Research* (2021) 23,4.

29   Nickolson Baker, Did the Coronavirus Escape from a Lab? *New York Magazine*, 4 January, 2021. James Rickards, *The New Great Depression: Winners and Losers in a Post-Pandemic World* (New York: Portfolio Penguin, 2021), pp. 15-26. See also Bret Weinstein: Why Covid-19 May Have Leaked from a Lab, the Joe Rogan Experience, 18 June 2020, online at https://www.youtube.com/watch?v=zQLF4DUSXGs

30   Andrew Lakoff, The Generic Biothreat, or, How We Became Unprepared, *Cultural Anthropology* (2008), 3, 3. The crisis was apparent by late January 2020; in many nations there was no public response until mid-March. King-wa Fu and Yuner Zhu, Did the world overlook the media's early warning of Covid-19? *Journal of Risk Research* (2020) 23, 7-8.

31   David Quammen, Why Weren't We Ready for the Coronavirus, *New Yorker*, 4 May, 2020; Damian Carrington, End destruction of nature to stop future pandemics, say scientists, *The Guardian*, 4 June, 2021. Melissa Davey, 'There are viruses just waiting in the wings': how do we stop the next pandemic? *The Guardian*, 18 June 2021.

32   Andreas Malm, *Corona, Climate, Chronic Emergency: War Communism in the Twenty-First Century*, London: Verso,

2020.

33 David Quammen, Why Weren't We Ready for the Coronavirus? *New Yorker*, 11 May 2020. 34 Jennifer Kahn, How Scientists Could Stop the Next Pandemic Before It Starts, *New York Times Magazine*, 21 April 2020.

35 Monitoring these news sites during the lockdown took 3 to 4 hours daily and a research diary kept during this time amounts to 90 pages of single-spaced notes.

36 Mike Davis, The Monster Enters, *New Left Review*, 122, March-April 2020, 8.

37 Susan Landau, Contact-Tracing Apps: What's Needed to Be an Effective Public Health Tool, Lawfare, 21 January 2021 online at: https://www.lawfareblog.com/contact-tracing-apps-whats-needed-be-effective-public-health-tool; Susan Landau, *People Count: Contact Tracing Apps and Public Health*, Cambridge: MIT Press, 2021.

38 However see, Dakshana Bascaramurty and others, How Covid-19 is exposing Canada's socioeconomic inequalities, *Globe and Mail,* 23 May 2020. The term *habitus* is from the sociology of Pierre Bourdieu and it attempts to capture individual experiences and social aspects of inequality and privilege.

39 Sarah Young, Zoombombing Your Toddler: User Experience and the Communication of Zoom's Privacy Crisis, *Journal of Business and Technical Communication* (2020) 35,1.

40 Natasha Singer and Nicole Perlroth, Zoom's Security Woes Were No Secret to Business Partners Like Dropbox, *New York Times,* 20 April 2020.

41 Interview with Tom Lamont, *The Guardian,* 1 August 2020.

42 Miles Kenyon, FAQ on Zoom Security, The Citizen Lab, 8 April 2020, online at https://citizenlab.ca/2020/04/faq-on-zoom-security-issues/

43 Steve Lohr, Companies That Rode Pandemic Boom Get a Reality Check, *New York Times*, 11 March 2021. David

Canellis, Zoom insiders dumped $119M in company stock this month, The Next Web, 24 June 2020, online at https://thenextweb.com/news/zoom-video-insiders-execs-stock-shares-sales-millions-june

44   Nicole Hong, Zoom Executive Accused of Disrupting Calls at China's Behest, *New York Times*, 18 December 2020. Microsoft provides a censored version of its search engine and other services in China. Paul Mozer, Microsoft's Bing Briefly Blocked 'Tank Man' Tiananmen Anniversary, *New York Times*, 5 June 2021. LinkedIn accounts may be blocked from view in China. Helen Davidson, LinkedIn blocks profiles from view in China if sensitive topics mentioned, *The Guardian*, 18 June 2021.

45   Alice Speri and Sam Biddle, Zoom censorship of Palestine seminars sparks fight over academic freedom, The Intercept, 14 November 2020.

46   Shoshana Zuboff, *The Age of Surveillance Capitalism: The Fight for a Human Future at the New Frontier of Power*. New York: Public Affairs, 2019.

47   S. Andrey, M. J. Masoodi, N. Malli, and S. Dorkenoo, *Mapping Toronto's Digital Divide*. Toronto: Ryerson, 2021. S. Craig Watkins and others, *The Digital Edge*, New York University Press, 2018 examines issues of the digital divide in schools. The Economic Policy Institute published a blog (17 April 2020) which describes economic differences in access to computers (one in four poor students do not have one) and home internet service.

48   Amber Joseph, What One Teacher Is Learning in a Pandemic, *New York Times*, 19 March 2020.

49   Tobias Jones, Italian lessons: what we've learned from 2 months of home schooling, *The Guardian*, 24 April 2020.

50   Caroline Alphonso, *Globe and Mail*, 28 April 2020.

51   Emma Beddington, *The Guardian*, 3 May 2020.

52   On the digital divide see Cevilia Kang, Desperate for Wi-

Fi, Many Have Nowhere to Go but a Parking Lot, *New York Times*, 5 May 2020, and David McCabe, Poor Americans Face Hurdles in Getting Promised Internet, *New York Times,* 20 May 2020. News reports occasionally suggest reviving school lessons on educational television because it is a more accessible medium than the internet.

53   For a summary of this international research see Pat Armstrong, Hugh Armstrong, Jacqueline Choiniere, Ruth Lowndes and James Struthers, *Re-imagining Long-term Residential Care in the Covid-19 Crisis*, Toronto, April 2020. See also Margaret J. McGregor and Lisa A. Ronald, *Residential Long-Term Care for Canadian Seniors Nonprofit, For-Profit or Does It Matter?* IRPP, January 2011.

54   Laura D. Allen and Liat Ayalon, 'It's Pure Panic': The Portrayal of Residential Care in American Newspapers During COVID-19, *Gerontologist* (2021) 61,1: 86–97.

55   Matthew Goldstein, Jessica Silver-Greenberg and Robert Gebeloff, Push for Profits Left Nursing Homes Struggling to Provide Care: Some with private equity owners, focused on making money, were particularly ill equipped and understaffed to handle Covid-19. *New York Times,* 7 May 2020. Marco Chown Oved and others, For-profit nursing homes have four times as many Covid-19 deaths as city-run homes, *Toronto Star*, 8 May, 2020.

56   Martin Regg Cohen, Doug Ford didn't protect long-term-care facilities from Covid-19; Neither did the rest of us, *Toronto Star*, 15 April 2020.

57   Editorial, The Guardian view on the care home crisis: culpable neglect, *The Guardian*, 5 May 2020.

58   The *New York Times* published an Opinion piece by Tobias L Millrood arguing that nursing homes had failed and Congress should not shield them from lawsuits over avoidable deaths. The *New York Times Magazine* published a useful overview by E Tammy Kim, This Is Why Nursing

Homes Failed So Badly, 31 December 2020.

59   For a summary of this research see Dennis Raphael, *Poverty in Canada*, Toronto: Canadian Scholars Press, 2020, Ch. 8 Poverty and Health.

60   Bryan Passifiume, City releases Toronto neighbourhood map of Covid-19 infections, *Toronto Star*, 27 May 2020.

61   Charles M, Blow, The Racial Time Bomb in the Covid-19 Crisis: Pre-existing health conditions leave one group particularly vulnerable, *New York Times,* 1 April 2020.

62   Dennis Raphael, Mainstream media and the social determinants of health: is it time to call it a day? *Health Promotion International* (2011) 26, 2: 220-229.

63   Kenyon Wallace, They've been called hot spots. It's actually 'code' for social inequity, *Toronto Star*, 11 May 2021.

64   For a critique of big-tech philanthropy see Nicole Ashoff, *The New Prophets of Capital,* London: Verso, 2015.

65   Erika Hayasaki, Amazon's Great Labor Awakening, *New York Times*, 18 February 2021; Jonathan Rothwell, How Social Class Affects Covid-Related Layoffs Worldwide, *New York Times*, 3 May 2021.

66   Rob Wallace and Roderick Wallace, Ebola's Ecologies: Agro-Economics and Epidemiology in West Africa, *New Left Review*, 102, Nov-Dec 2016.

67   Andrew Lakoff, The Generic Biothreat, or, How We Became Unprepared, *Cultural Anthropology* (2008), 3, 3.

68   Kathy Tomlinson and Grant Robertson, Ottawa had a playbook for a coronavirus-like pandemic 14 years ago. What went wrong? *Globe and Mail*, 9 April 2020.

69   Kevin Quealy, The Richest Neighborhoods Emptied Out Most as Coronavirus Hit New York City. *New York Times*, 15 May 2020. See also, Norimitsu Onishi and Constant Méheut, Rich Europeans Flee Virus for 2nd Homes, Spreading Fear and Fury; In France and the rest of Europe, the affluent decamp cities to spend their confinement in

vacation homes, widening class divides. *New York Times*, 29 March 2020.

70 For a comparative study of the *New York Times, Washington Post*, BuzzFeed and VICE, see Jill Abramson, *Merchants of Truth: The Business of News and the Fight for Facts*. New York: Simon & Schuster, 2019. On *The Guardian*'s adaption to the world of online news see Alan Rusbridger, *Breaking News: The Remaking of Journalism and Why It Matters Now*. New York: Farrar, Straus and Giroux, 2018.

71 'We did it to ourselves': scientist says intrusion into nature led to pandemic, *The Guardian*, 25 April 2020.

72 *New Left Review*, 122, March-April 2020; Robert Brenner, Escalating Plunder, *New Left Review*, 123, May-June 2020.

73 David Quammen, Why Weren't We Ready for the Coronavirus? *New Yorker*, 4 May 2020.

74 The *New Yorker* was also one of the few media to pay attention to Mike Davis, author of *The Monster at Our Door*, publishing a profile of him by Dana Goodyear, *New Yorker*, 24 April 2020.

75 Yang and Allen, Leaked email reveals Ontario regional medical officer's criticism of provincial Covid-19 strategy as cracks emerge in front line, *Toronto Star*, 20 March 2020. Much later, in early 2021, the *Star* also published a series of investigative articles on long-term residences.

76 For the conservative editorial position on this issue see Cliff Taylor, How are we going to pay for the Irish big state utopia? *Irish Times*, 25 April 2020.

77 VICE News, Amazon Leak, April 2, 2020; VICE News, They Call Me a Hero Because I Work at Kroger, So Why Do I Feel Disposable? 15 May 2020. Andrea Park, Asian Americans Are Dealing with a Wave of Bigotry and Assaults Because of Coronavirus, VICE, 19 May 2020. Nafeez Ahmed, Covid-19 Is a Symptom of a Planet That's Been Pushed Past a Tipping Point, VICE, 23 November 2020 stands out as an

exceptional in-depth report.

78   William B. Karesh and Robert A. Cook, The Human-Animal Link, *Foreign Affairs*, July/August 2005. For the effects of factory farming on human bodies see Alex Blanchette, *Porkpolis: American Animality, Standardized Life, and the Factory Farm* (Durham: Duke University Press, 2020) and Oxfam America, Disposable: In the face of Covid-19, the poultry industry seems willing to pay for cheap chicken with worker's lives (2021), online at https://webassets.oxfamamerica.org/media/documents/Disposable_Poultry_COVID.pdf

79   Michael Pollan, The Sickness in Our Food Supply, *New York Review of Books*, 11 June 2020; Megan Molteni, Why Meatpacking Plants Have Become Covid-19 Hot Spots, *Wired*, 7 May 2020.

80   David Quammen, And Then the Gorillas Started Coughing: Humans are spreading the coronavirus to other animals, *New York Times*, 19 February 2021; Joanne M Santini and Sarah J L Edwards, Host range of SARS-CoV-2 and implications for public health, the *Lancet*, August 2020.

81   We're modern slaves, *The Guardian*, 2 May 2020.

82   Bibi van der Zee and others, 'Chaotic and crazy': meat plants around the world struggle with virus outbreaks, *The Guardian*, 11 May 2020.

83   Ella McSweeney, 'Everyone's on top of you, sneezing and coughing': life inside Ireland's meat plants, *The Guardian*, 14 May 2020.

84   The *Irish Times*, 8 May 2020.

85   Simon Carswell, Inside a Covid-19 outbreak at a meatpacking plant, *Irish Times*, 16 May 2020.

86   Migrant workers angry over lack of Covid-19 protection in meat plants, *Irish Times*, 10 July 2020. The *Irish Times* then reported on conditions for these low-paid workers, 28 July 2020.

87 Anna Swanson and others, Pork Chops vs. People: Battling Coronavirus in an Iowa Meat Plant, *New York Times*, 10 May 2020. Michael Corkery and others, As Meatpacking Plants Reopen, Data About Worker Illness Remains Elusive, *New York Times*, 25 May 2020. Jazmine Hughes, As Meatpacking Plants Look to Reopen, Some Families are Wary, *New York Times*, 28 May 2020. The *Times* also published an opinion piece by Richard Trumka, president of the AFL-CIO, If Trump Wants Meat Plants Open, He Should Protect Their Workers, *New York Times*, 7 May 2020.

88 Carrie Tait and others, Cargill shuts down Quebec plant after 64 workers test positive for Covid-19, *Globe and Mail*, 11 May 2020. Tavia Grant and others, Cargill meat plant, site of Canada's largest Covid-19 outbreak, prepares to reopen, *Globe and Mail*, 3 May 2020. Kathryn Blaze Baum and others, Ottawa earmarks $77-million to protect meat plant workers, but union says it misses mark, *Globe and Mail*, 5 May 2020. The *Toronto Star* did cover this story at the time, though often relying on news agency reports.

89 Amy Mitchell and others, Americans Who Mainly Get Their News on Social Media Are Less Engaged, Less Knowledgeable, Pew Research Center, July 2020. Philipp Muller and others, Appetizer or main dish? Explaining the use of Facebook news posts as a substitute for other news sources, *Computers in Human Behavior* (2016) 65:431-441, finds that frequent scanning of news on Facebook can lead to a false sense of being informed. There are knowledge gaps between high-education and low-education users of Facebook.

90 Nic Newman and others, *Digital News Report*, Reuters Institute, 2020 online at: https://www.digitalnewsreport. org

91 Marc Tracy, News Media Outlets Have Been Ravaged by the Pandemic, *New York Times*, 10 April 2020. Michael

Barthel and others, Coronavirus-Driven Downturn Hits Newspapers Hard as TV New Thrives, Pew Research Center, October 2020. Michael Luo, The Fate of the News in the Age of Coronavirus, *New Yorker*, 29 March 2020. Kristen Hare, The coronavirus has closed more than 70 local newsrooms across America, Poynter, 8 June 2021, online https://www.poynter.org/locally/2021/the-coronavirus-has-closed-more-than-60-local-newsrooms-across-america-and-counting/

92 Jane Martinson in *The Guardian*, 15 May 2020.

93 Josh Rubin, Torstar to be sold, taken private in $52-million deal, *Toronto Star*, 26 May 2020.

94 Pew Research Center, *Coronavirus-Driven Downturn Hits Newspapers Hard as TV News Thrives*, October 2020. Online.

95 Andre Picard, 'We have to test and trace more to end lockdowns safely', *Globe and Mail,* 22 May 2020.

96 A dispute in February 2020 about asymptomatic people shedding the virus illustrates the relationship between politics and medical research. Dr Camilla Roth from Germany described in the *New England Journal of Medicine* evidence of infection from an asymptomatic contact. A competing German team published a full article in the *Lancet*. The evidence of Dr Roth was disputed in an article in *Science*, and this article was widely cited on social media by people opposed to public health measures to contain the virus. Matt Apuzzo and others, How the World Missed Covis-19's Silent Spread, *New York Times*, 27 June 2020.

97 Dr Peter Juni from The Ontario COVID-19 Science Advisory Table. Later in the crisis, Dr Juni started to be much more critical of the Ontario government.

98 Doctors for Justice in LTC, online at https://docs4ltcjustice.ca

99 Nickolson Baker, Did the Coronavirus Escape From a Lab? *New York Magazine*, 4 January 2021. Lily Kuo, Wuhan lab

says its bat strains were not Covid-19, *The Guardian*, 24 May 2020. AFP-Geneva, Covid probably passed to humans from bats via other animal, finds WHO report, *The Guardian*, 29 March 2021.

100 Johan Lindell and Jan Fredrik Hovden, Distinctions in the media welfare state: audience fragmentation in post-egalitarian Sweden, *Media, Culture & Society* (2018) 40,5: 639-655.

101 Ontario Nurses' Association Says Contract Talks for Hospital Registered Nurses Have Broken Down, 4 March 2020. Online at: https://www.ona.org/news-posts/20200304-hospital-bargaining/

102 Anonymous, I'm an NHS doctor – and I've had enough of people clapping for me: The health service is not a charity and it is not staffed by heroes. It has been run into the ground by successive governments. The *Guardian*, 21 May 2020. See also, Shan Mohammed and others, The 'nurse as hero' discourse in the Covid-19 pandemic: A poststructural discourse analysis, *International Journal of Nursing Studies*, January 2021.

103 There is some evidence that this myth was wearing thin as the pandemic went on. During the second wave in December 2020 to January 2021 there was considerable criticism in the news media of the Ontario government for removing sick days introduced by the prior government, and inadequate testing and contact tracing. The Ford government put the responsibility on individuals to 'stay at home' while permitting a long list of exceptions for employers to continue economic activities. By January 2021 over 3000 residents of long-term homes had died from Covid-19. Zena Salem, Ontario surpasses grim milestone of 3,000 deaths in long-term care since pandemic began, with 34 more reported, *Toronto Star*, 13 January 2021.

104 There was even a punk-rock song about SARS by Career

Suicide, a Toronto hardcore band, on Deranged Records in 2003. You can listen to their song 'Quarantined' on YouTube https://www.youtube.com/watch?v=9YJXk8sjeAk

105 Mike Davis, *The Monster Enters* (2020), 39.

106 Ai Xiaming, Wuhan Diary, *New Left Review*, 122 (Mar/April 2020). *Wuhan, Wuhan*, dir. Yueng Chang, RealDoc Productions, 2021.

107 Rob Wallace, Notes on a novel Coronavirus, online at https://mronline.org/2020/01/29/notes-on-a-novel-coronavirus/

108 King-wa Fu and Yuner Zhu, Did the world overlook the media's early warning of Covid-19? *Journal of Risk Research* (2020) 23, 7-8. Michael Lewis, *The Premonition: A Pandemic Story* (New York: Norton, 2021).

109 Raymond Williams, Base and Superstructure in Marxist Cultural Theory, in his *Problems in Materialism and Culture,* London: Verso, 1980, 31-49.

110 Nafeez Ahmed, Deforestation and the Risk of Collapse: Reframing Covid-19 as a Planetary Boundary Effect, The Schumacher Institute, 2020. Andreas Malm, *Corona, Climate, Chronic Emergency: War Communism in the Twenty-First Century*, London: Verso, 2020.

111 Apoorva Mandavilli, Reaching 'Herd Immunity' Is Unlikely in the US, Experts Now Believe, *New York Times*, 3 May 2021.

112 Adam Tooze, We are living through the first economic crisis of the Anthropocene, *The Guardian*, 7 May 2020. Eyal Press, Safety Last: In a pandemic, Labor Secretary Eugene Scalia is weakening worker protections, *New Yorker*, 26 October 2020.

113 Larry Brilliant interviewed on *The Current*, CBC Radio 1, 15 March 2021.

114 The section on the economy is one of the weakest parts of Lawrence Wright, The Plague Year, *New Yorker,* 4 January 2021.

115 For an example of this kind of reporting see, Matina Stevis-Gridneff and Jack Ewing, EU Is Facing Its Worst Recession Ever. Watch Out, World.

116 Editorial, *Globe and Mail*, 28 April 2020.

117 Adam Tooze, Should we be scared of the coronavirus debt mountain? *The Guardian*, 27 April 2020. Reports by Larry Elliott in *The Guardian* sometimes went beyond macroeconomic statistics to describe how the pandemic is affecting low-paid workers.

118 Matt Phillips, How the Government Pulls Coronavirus Relief Money Out of Thin Air, *New York Times*, 15 April 2020.

119 Adam Tooze, How coronavirus almost brought down the global financial system, *The Guardian*, 14 April 2020.

120 Joseph E. Stiglitz, A Lasting Remedy for the Covid-19 Pandemic's Economic Crisis, New York Review of Books Daily, 8 April 2020. Online at: https://www.nybooks.com/daily/2020/04/08/a-lasting-remedy-for-the-covid-19-pandemics-economic-crisis/

121 Robert Brenner, Escalating Plunder, *New Left Review,* May-June 2020. Relevant news reports include: Jessica Silver-Greenberg, Jesse Drucker and David Enrich report on apparent abuse of government bailouts: Hospitals Got Bailouts and Furloughed Thousands While Paying CEOs Millions, *New York Times*, 6 May 2020. Emily Holden, Fossil fuel firms linked to Trump get millions in coronavirus small business aid, *The Guardian*, 1 May 2020. Peter Stone, Trump's wealthy friends look to cash in during coronavirus crisis, *The Guardian*, 3 May 2020. Emily Holden, Revealed: long-troubled US oil firms are capitalizing on coronavirus assistance, *The Guardian*, 14 May 2020. Matt Phillips, Too Big to Fail: The Entire Private Sector, *New York Times*, 19 May 2020. Nicholas Kristof, Crumbs for the Hungry but Windfalls for the Rich, *New York Times*, 23 May 2020. Jesse

Drucker and others, Wealthiest Hospitals Got Billions in Bailout for Struggling Health Providers, *New York Times*, 25 May 2020.

122 *The Guardian* published an interview with Thomas Piketty, 12 May 2020 which briefly discusses issues of social inequality and the prospects for radical social change.

123 Grace Blakeley, *The Corona Crash: How the Pandemic will change Capitalism* (London Verso, 2020).

124 Rebecca Robbins and Peter S. Goodman, Pfizer Reaps Hundreds of Millions in Profits from Covid Vaccine, *New York Times*, 4 May 2021. Chris Hamby and Sheryl Gay Stolberg, How One Firm Put an 'Extraordinary Burden' on the US's Troubled Stockpile, *New York Times*, 6 March 2021.

125 Emily Flitter and Stacy Cowley, Banks Gave Richest Clients 'Concierge Treatment' for Pandemic Aid, *New York Times*, 22 April 2020.

126 Max Horkheimer and Theodor W. Adorno, *Dialectic of Enlightenment*, trans. Edmund Jephcott (Stanford: Stanford University Press, 2002). For warnings about economic crisis and political authoritarianism see Wolfgang Streeck, *Buying Time: The Delayed Crisis of Democratic Capitalism*, 2nd ed. (London: Verso 2007).

Further Reading

News Media

Abramson, Jill (2019) *Merchants of Truth: The Business of News and the Fight for Facts.* New York: Simon & Schuster.

Basch, Corey H. and Aleksander Kecojic and Victoria H. Wagner, Coverage of the Covid-19 Pandemic in Online Versions of Highly Circulated US Daily Newspapers, *Journal of Community Health* 45 (2020): 1089-1097.

Benkler, Yochai, Faris, Robert and Roberts, Hal (2018) *Network Propaganda: Manipulation, Disinformation, and Radicalization in American Politics.* Oxford: Oxford University Press.

Blakely, Debra E. (2003) Social Construction of Three Influenza Pandemics in the New York Times. *Journalism and Mass Communication Quarterly* (80) 4: 884-898.

Bourdieu, Pierre (1998) *On Television.* New York: The New Press.

Faris, Robert and others, *Polarization and the Pandemic: American Political Discourse March-May 2020.* Berkman Klein Center for Internet & Society Research, October 2020.

Friel, Howard and Falk, Richard (2004) *The Record of the Paper: How the New York Times Misrepresents US Foreign Policy.* London and New York: Verso.

Gorman, Brian (2015) *Crash to Paywall: Canadian Newspapers and the Great Disruption.* Montreal and Kingston: McGill-Queens University Press.

Hallin, Dan (1989) *The 'Uncensored War': The Media and Vietnam.* Berkeley and Los Angeles: University of California Press.

Herman, Edward S. and Chomsky, Noam (2002) *Manufacturing Consent: The Political Economy of the Mass Media.* New York: Pantheon Books.

Lindell, Johan and Hovden, Jan Fredrik (2018) 'Distinctions in the media welfare state: audience fragmentation in post-egalitarian Sweden', *Media, Culture & Society*, 40(5): 639-655.

Mai, Quan D. (2016) All the labor problems fit to print: the New York Times and the cultural production of the US 'labor problem', 1870-1932. *Labour History* 57(2): 141-169.

Peck, Reece (2019) *Fox Populism: Branding Conservatism as Working Class*. Cambridge: Cambridge University Press.

Raphael, Dennis (2011) Mainstream media and the social determinants of health in Canada: is it time to call it a day? *Health Promotion International* (26)2: 220-229.

Robinson, Piers and others, *Pockets of Resistance: British News media, War and Theory in the 2003 Invasion of Iraq*. Manchester: Manchester University Press, 2010.

Rusbridger, Alan (2018) *Breaking News: The Remaking of Journalism and Why It Matters Now*. New York: Farrar, Straus and Giroux.

Covid-19 Pandemic

Ahmed, Nafeez (2020) *Deforestation and the Risk of Collapse: Reframing Covid-19 as a Planetary Boundary Effect*. The Schumacher Institute, 2020. Online.

Blakeley, Grace (2020) *The Corona Crash: How the Pandemic will change Capitalism*. London and New York: Verso.

Brenner, Robert. Escalating Plunder, *New Left Review*, May-June 2020.

Davis, Mike (2005) *The Monster at Our Door: The Global Threat of Avian Flu*. New York: The New Press. Reprinted with additional material as *The Monster Enters: Covid-19, Avian Flu and the Plagues of Capitalism*, OR Books, 2020.

Foreign Affairs (2020) *The Next Pandemic: Why the World Was Not Prepared for Covid-19*. Foreign Affairs Anthology.

Landau, Susan (2021) *People Count: Contract-Tracing Apps and Public Health*. MIT Press.

Lewis, Michael (2021) *The Premonition: A Pandemic Story*, New York: Norton, 2021.

MacGillis, Alec (2021) *Fulfillment: Winning and Losing in One-Click America.* New York: Farrar, Straus and Giroux, 2021.

Malm, Andreas (2020) *Corona, Climate, Chronic Emergency: War Communism in the Twentieth-First Century*, London: Verso.

New Left Review (2020) 'A Planetary Pandemic' special issue of *New Left Review* 122, March / April 2020.

Picard, Andre (2021) *Neglected No More: The Urgent Need to Improve the Lives of Canada's*

Elders in the Wake of a Pandemic. Random House Canada.

Quammen, David (2020) Why Weren't We Ready for the Coronavirus? *New Yorker,* 4 May.

Surveillance & Society (2021) 19(1). Special issue on *Surveillance and the COVID-19 Pandemic: Views from Around the World.*

Wright, Lawrence (2021) The Plague Year, *New Yorker*, Jan 4.

CULTURE, SOCIETY & POLITICS

The modern world is at an impasse. Disasters scroll across our smartphone screens and we're invited to like, follow or upvote, but critical thinking is harder and harder to find. Rather than connecting us in common struggle and debate, the internet has sped up and deepened a long-standing process of alienation and atomization. Zer0 Books wants to work against this trend. With critical theory as our jumping off point, we aim to publish books that make our readers uncomfortable. We want to move beyond received opinions.

Zer0 Books is on the left and wants to reinvent the left. We are sick of the injustice, the suffering and the stupidity that defines both our political and cultural world, and we aim to find a new foundation for a new struggle.

If this book has helped you to clarify an idea, solve a problem or extend your knowledge, you may want to check out our online content as well. Look for Zer0 Books: Advancing Conversations in the iTunes directory and for our Zer0 Books YouTube channel.

Popular videos include:
Žižek and the Double Blackmain
The Intellectual Dark Web is a Bad Sign
Can there be an Anti-SJW Left?
Answering Jordan Peterson on Marxism

Follow us on Facebook
at https://www.facebook.com/ZeroBooks and Twitter at https://
twitter.com/Zer0Books

Bestsellers from Zer0 Books include:

Give Them An Argument
Logic for the Left
Ben Burgis
Many serious leftists have learned to distrust talk of logic. This is a serious mistake.
Paperback: 978-1-78904-210-8 ebook: 978-1-78904-211-5

Poor but Sexy
Culture Clashes in Europe East and West
Agata Pyzik
How the East stayed East and the West stayed West.
Paperback: 978-1-78099-394-2 ebook: 978-1-78099-395-9

An Anthropology of Nothing in Particular
Martin Demant Frederiksen
A journey into the social lives of meaninglessness.
Paperback: 978-1-78535-699-5 ebook: 978-1-78535-700-8

In the Dust of This Planet
Horror of Philosophy vol. 1
Eugene Thacker
In the first of a series of three books on the Horror of Philosophy, *In the Dust of This Planet* offers the genre of horror as a way of thinking about the unthinkable.
Paperback: 978-1-84694-676-9 ebook: 978-1-78099-010-1

The End of Oulipo?
An Attempt to Exhaust a Movement
Lauren Elkin, Veronica Esposito
Paperback: 978-1-78099-655-4 ebook: 978-1-78099-656-1

Capitalist Realism
Is There No Alternative?
Mark Fisher
An analysis of the ways in which capitalism has presented itself
as the only realistic political-economic system.
Paperback: 978-1-84694-317-1 ebook: 978-1-78099-734-6

Ghosts of My Life
Writings on Depression, Hauntology and Lost Futures
Mark Fisher
Paperback: 978-1-78099-226-6 ebook: 978-1-78279-624-4

Kill All Normies
Angela Nagle
Online culture wars from 4chan and Tumblr to Trump.
Paperback: 978-1-78535-543-1 ebook: 978-1-78535-544-8

Cartographies of the Absolute
Alberto Toscano, Jeff Kinkle
An aesthetics of the economy for the twenty-first century.
Paperback: 978-1-78099-275-4 ebook: 978-1-78279-973-3

Malign Velocities
Accelerationism and Capitalism
Benjamin Noys
Long listed for the Bread and Roses Prize 2015, *Malign Velocities*
argues against the need for speed, tracking acceleration
as the symptom of the ongoing crises of capitalism.
Paperback: 978-1-78279-300-7 ebook: 978-1-78279-299-4

Babbling Corpse
Vaporwave and the Commodification of Ghosts
Grafton Tanner
Paperback: 978-1-78279-759-3 ebook: 978-1-78279-760-9

Meat Market
Female Flesh under Capitalism
Laurie Penny
A feminist dissection of women's bodies as the fleshy fulcrum of capitalist cannibalism, whereby women are both consumers and consumed.
Paperback: 978-1-84694-521-2 ebook: 978-1-84694-782-7

New Work New Culture
Work we want and a culture that strengthens us
Frithjof Bergmann
A serious alternative for mankind and the planet.
Paperback: 978-1-78904-064-7 ebook: 978-1-78904-065-4

Romeo and Juliet in Palestine
Teaching Under Occupation
Tom Sperlinger
Life in the West Bank, the nature of pedagogy and the role of a university under occupation.
Paperback: 978-1-78279-637-4 ebook: 978-1-78279-636-7

Rebel Rebel
Chris O'Leary
David Bowie: every single song. Everything you want to know, everything you didn't know.
Paperback: 978-1-78099-244-0 ebook: 978-1-78099-713-1

Sweetening the Pill
or How We Got Hooked on Hormonal Birth Control
Holly Grigg-Spall
Has contraception liberated or oppressed women?
Sweetening the Pill breaks the silence on the dark side of hormonal contraception.
Paperback: 978-1-78099-607-3 ebook: 978-1-78099-608-0

Why Are We The Good Guys?
Reclaiming Your Mind from the Delusions of Propaganda
David Cromwell
A provocative challenge to the standard ideology that Western power is a benevolent force in the world.
Paperback: 978-1-78099-365-2 ebook: 978-1-78099-366-9

The Writing on the Wall
On the Decomposition of Capitalism and its Critics
Anselm Jappe, Alastair Hemmens
A new approach to the meaning of social emancipation.
Paperback: 978-1-78535-581-3 ebook: 978-1-78535-582-0

Enjoying It
Candy Crush and Capitalism
Alfie Bown
A study of enjoyment and of the enjoyment of studying. Bown asks what enjoyment says about us and what we say about enjoyment, and why.
Paperback: 978-1-78535-155-6 ebook: 978-1-78535-156-3

Color, Facture, Art and Design
Iona Singh
This materialist definition of fine-art develops guidelines for architecture, design, cultural-studies and ultimately social change.
Paperback: 978-1-78099-629-5 ebook: 978-1-78099-630-1

Most titles are published in paperback and as an ebook. Paperbacks are available in traditional bookshops. Both print and ebook formats are available online.
Follow us on Facebook
at https://www.facebook.com/ZeroBooks
and Twitter at https://twitter.com/Zer0Books